THE
SCOUT
RIDDLE
BOOK

A collection of jokes and riddles related to Scouting, camping, and hiking

Thomas Mercaldo

Illustrations: Thomas C. Mercaldo and Haruthay Rasmidatta
Cover Design: Haruthay Rasmidatta

Printed in the United States.
Nineth Printing - Anniversary Edition

Aquinas Scout Books
C/O Thomas C. Mercaldo
154 Herbert Street
Milford, CT 06461

Scout Fun Books is not officially affiliated with the Boy Scouts of America, Girl Scouts of America, Scouts Canada or the World Organization of Scouting.

Scout Fun Books can be purchased on a wholesale basis for resale in Camp Stores, Scout Shops and Trading Posts. For details write to us at the above address or contact us by email at BoyScoutBooks@aol.com.

Preface

As you read this page, somewhere on this planet, there is a Scout huddled around a campfire, firing off his favorite puns. This book was written in honor of such Scouts; Scouts in the heart of the wilderness in search of good clean fun. The Scout Riddle Book features hundreds of jokes and riddles; humor that can be enjoyed by both young and old. I hope this publication adds to the fun associated with your next Scouting event.

Tom Mercaldo

P.S. This expanded Anniversary Edition Scout Riddle Book contains even more Scout Jokes and Riddles than the original edition.

Table of Contents

Scout Craft

Why can't the mountain climber ever improve?
Because he's reached his peak.

Why did Joe Scout cook beef in his tent?
He wanted to have tent steaks.

What happened to the Scout who refinished the wooden flagpole?
He varnished into thin air.

You go camping and you only have one match. On arriving at the cabin you find a wood burning stove in one corner, a kerosene lantern in another corner and a candle in the third corner. What would you light first?
The match.

What do you get when you cross poison ivy and a four leaf clover?
A rash of good luck.

What do you call a small canvas doghouse?
A pup tent.

What's the best way to carve wood?
Whittle by whittle.

Why shouldn't the Scouts at camp swim on an empty stomach?
Because it's easier to swim on water.

Why did the Scout stuff dollar bills in his shoe?
He wanted to have a legal tender foot.

Why didn't the Cub Scout wear any clothes?
Because he was a bear (bare).

What badge do you earn for greeting royalty?
Hi King

Scout Lore

What is brown and furry and bothers Scouts about earning more awards?

A merit badger.

What member of the troop is responsible for keeping track of 25 cent pieces?

The Quartermaster.

What do you call a small cat that puts band aids on cuts?

A first aid kit.

Who in the troop gives an explanation of what things look like?

De Scribe.

What is the best way to start a fire with two sticks?

Make sure one of the sticks is a match.

Where will campers sleep in the 25th century?

In the future tents.

Why did Joe Scout mail himself to the awards ceremony?

He wanted to become First Class.

Did you hear about the new Scout camera?

It only takes slides (remove the neckerchief slide of the Scout you are talking to while telling this joke).

I know a Scout who thinks he's an owl.

When the Scout asks "Who?", answer, make that two Scouts that think they're owls.

Why was the Scout afraid to walk on the rocks?

He was a tenderfoot.

What do you call an Eagle Scout with a crew cut?

A bald eagle.

What do playing cards and cub scouts have in common?

They both belong to a pack.

What organization did the cavemen establish to teach their kids to hunt?

The Club Scouts.

A boy walked into a restaurant and ordered apple pie al a mode and an ice cream soda. The waitress knew at once that he was a boy scout. How did she know?

He had his Scout uniform on.

What do British Scouts call six cans of Eagle gasoline at a campfire?

The Eagle petrol.

What merit badge do you earn for getting your ears pierced in China?

Orient-earring.

What happened to the Scout who put a firecracker in the pancake batter?

When the pancakes came, he blew his stack.

What's green, lies on the ground, and is covered with cookie crumbs?

A Girl Scout who has fainted.

What's the difference between Mars and a Girl Scout camporee?

There might be intelligent life on Mars.

What do you call a Girl Scout glued to the ceiling?

Stuck up.

How do you know when a Girl Scout has been baking cookies?

You find M&M shells all over the kitchen floor..

What do you call a Cub Scout holding a frisbee?

A cub and saucer

How are a bad boy and a canoe alike?

They both get paddled.

In what month do Girl Scouts talk the least?

February.

Why did the Scoutleader plan a parade for 3/4/2099?
He wanted the troops to March forth in the future.

Why wasn't the Girl Scout afraid when the lion escaped from the zoo?
She heard it was a man eating lion.

Did you hear the joke about the rope?
Skip it.

How do postcards rank with Scouts?
They're first class.

What did the kindling wood say to the fireplace?
Goodbye, I've met my match.

What happened to the match that lost its temper?
It flared up.

What happened to the patrol that played with matches?
They made complete ashes of themselves.

What do you call a hill that scouts cook their meals on?
A mountain range.

What was Jester's favorite cereal before he became an Eagle?
Life.

What kind of knots do Scouts tie in space?
Astro-knots.

What planet has the most Scouts?
Earth.

Why did the Scout salute the refrigerator?
It was a General Electric.

Did you hear about the tenderfoot who wrote an essay about his compass?
He called it his compassition.

What happened to the Scout who wanted to be a piece of firewood?
He made a fuel of himself.

What do you call a boomerang that doesn't return?
A stick.

How far did Sylvester Stallone advance in Scouting?
All the way to Star.

What type of trees do Eagle Scouts plant in Hawaii?
Eagle palms.

What do you call it when a Scout promises to be faithful to furniture polish?
Pledge Allegiance.

What rank was the new teacher?
First class.

Why was the teacher sad on his second day at school?
He went back to second class.

What did the Scoutmaster say when he found Riley's lost life award?
That's the life of Riley.

Why did the British Scouts get 2 dollars worth of gasoline?
They needed a new petrol liter.

What happened to the Scout who ironed a four leaf clover?
He really pressed his luck.

Why was the dumb Scout afraid of the police?
Because he broke one of the Scout laws.

Scout Camp

Why did the insect eat on the tent flap?
>*It was a dining fly.*

What do you get when you cross a brook and a stream?
>*Wet feet.*

What do you get when you cross a baseball player with a boy scout?
>*A boy who likes to pitch tents.*

What does it mean when the barometer is falling?
>*The Scout that nailed it up didn't do a good job.*

How did the Scout feel when he came out of the woods?
>*Bushed.*

What do they do at Scout camp when it rains?
>*Let it rain.*

Can you drop a full canteen without spilling any water?
>*Yes, if the canteen is filled with soda.*

What did the father buffalo say to his son when he was leaving Scout camp?
>*Bye Son (Bison).*

How do you make a fire lighter?
>*Take off one log.*

What do you call it when you bring the king camping and he climbs a mountain?
>*HiKing.*

How do you avoid getting sick from insect bites while camping?
>*Don't bite any insects.*

What did the Scout do with the tree after he chopped it down?
>*He chopped it up.*

Why do the beavers at camp turn in a circle before going to bed?
They try to do a good turn daily.

If there is a kidnapping at camp what should you do?
Wake him up.

What does it mean when you find a horseshoe at camp?
Some poor horse is going around barefoot.

Why did the Scout troop invite Nolan Ryan to go camping?
They needed someone to pitch the tents.

Where do backpackers keep their sleeping bags?
In their nap sacks(Knapsacks).

Where is it best to find books about the trees at camp?
A branch Library.

How do you make a hot dog stand in the middle of the woods?
Steal his chair.

Why don't elephants bring backpacks to Scout camp?
They keep everything in their trunks.

Why did the ghost stop scaring the scouts at camp?
His haunting license expired.

At camp, what rises in the morning and waves all day?
The American Flag.

Does camp have both hot and cold water?
Yes. Cold in the winter, and hot in the summer.

What insect sits in a circle of rocks blinking its tailight?
A Camp Fire Fly.

What did the Quarterback say to the Scout troop?
Hike.

Why were all the baby ants at camp confused?
Because all of their uncles were ants.

The Wild Adirondack Cow

For those who do not live in the Northeast, this section requires a special introduction. The Wild Adirondack Cow is a carnivorous Moose-like creature that inhabited the Adirondack and Berkshire valleys. Similar to a Holstein in shape and color, the much larger Wild Adirondack Cow features a wide jaw and bear-like teeth. Scientists believe the Wild Adirondack Cow (WAC) is now extinct; nonetheless, many campers claim to have seen the creature in recent times. Tales about this vicious relative of the grizzly bear are a central theme in Indian folklore and camp tradition.

Why shouldn't you cry if a Wild Adirondack Cow falls on the ice?
Because there is no use crying over spilled milk.

Why shouldn't you cry over spilled milk?
It will get too salty.

What happens to a Wild Adirondack Cow when it stands out in the rain?
It gets wet.

Where can you find Wild Adirondack Cow artifacts?
In a Moo-seum.

Were Wild Adirondack Cows cannibalistic?
Yes, many were known to eat there fodder.

Do you know how long Wild Adirondack Cows should be milked?
The same as short Wild Adirondack Cows.

What would you get if you feed a Wild Adirondack Cow $100 dollar bills?
You'd get rich milk.

Why was the Wild Adirondack Cow afraid?
Because he was a Cow-ard.

Why did the Indians place bells on Wild Adirondack Cows?
Because their horns don't work.

What do you call a Wild Adirondack Cow with no ears?
Whatever you want; he can't hear you.

What did the Eskimos call the northern relative of the Wild Adirondack Cow?
The Wild Eski-MOO's.

Where did the Wild Adirondack Cow go when he lost his tail?
To a retail store.

What made the Wild Adirondack Cow's dreams come true?
His dairy God-mother.

What do you call a Wild Adirondack Cow that can't give milk?
An udder failure.

What did one Wild Adirondack Cow say to the other?
Nothing, Wild Adirondack Cows can't talk.

Where does a Wild Adirondack Cow go for entertainment?
To the mooovies.

When should Wild Adirondack Cows blow their horns?
When they're stuck in traffic.

What do you call Wild Adirondack Cows that ride on trains?
Passengers.

What does See O double you stand for?
Cow.

How do you keep a Wild Adirondack Cow from charging?
Take away his credit card.

What did the Wild Adirondack Cow say after eating a DVD?
I liked the book better.

What would you call it if a Wild Adirondack Cow helped perform surgery?
Cow-operation.

What do Wild Adirondack Cows have that no other animal has?
Wild Adirondack Calves.

What is black and white and blue all over?
A Wild Adirondack Cow at the north pole.

What is black and white and blue and hides in caves?
A Wild Adirondack Cow that's afraid of polar bears.

What do you call a Wild Adirondack Cow at the north pole?
Lost.

What is black and white, black and white, black and white, and yellow?
Three Wild Adirondack Cows eating a banana.

What is black and white and red all over?
A newspaper.

Why can't you teach a Wild Adirondack Cow to dance?
Because it has two left feet.

Why did the astronauts find bones on the moon?
The first cow didn't make it.

What happens to Wild Adirondack Cows that stay in the pasture all night?
They get pasteurized.

Why don't many Wild Adirondack Cows go to college?
Because not many graduate from high school.

What do you call a sleeping male WAC?
A bull-dozer.

Why does a WAC kneel before it attacks?
Because it is preying.

A Wild Adirondack Cow is tied to a rope 8 feet long. A bale of hay is 24 feet 5 inches away, and the Wild Adirondack Cow wants to eat the hay. How can he do it?

He can just walk over and eat it. The rope isn't tied to anything.

What kind of sandwiches do female Wild Adirondack Cows like?

Bull-only.

What type of coffee do mother WAC's drink?

De-calf-inated.

Why did the Wild Adirondack Cow say, "Baa, baa?"

He was trying to learn a second language.

How do you make a Wild Adirondack Cow stew?

Leave him waiting for 5 or 6 hours.

Why did the Wild Adirondack Cow cross the road?

It was the chicken's day off.

Why did the Wild Adirondack Cow cross the highway?

To prove he wasn't chicken.

What's black and white and green?

A seasick Wild Adirondack Cow.

What's black and white and blue?

An extremely sad Wild Adirondack Cow.

What's black and white and black and blue?

A Wild Adirondack Cow that fell down a hill.

What do you say to a Wild Adirondack Cow that gets in your way?

MOOOve over.

Why did the Wild Adirondack Cow change his socks on the golf course?

He got a hole in one.

A Wild Adirondack Cow with large black spots married a Wild Adirondack Cow with small black spots. Their first son had no spots. What did they call him?

Harold.

Where do young Wild Adirondack Cows eat lunch?

In a calf-ateria.

What Cow baseball player holds the most milk?

The pitcher.

Where do you find Wild Adirondack Cows that are waiting to get into the game?

In the bull-pen.

What did the Wild Adirondack Cow wear on his head during the baseball game?

A baseball cap.

Wild Adirondack Cow attack survival guide

1. Use the buddy system. If a Wild Adirondack cow attacks, push your buddy toward the cow.
2. Hold up a large mirror to the WAC, he'll think he's being attacked.
3. Carry a 50 gallon milking machine with you at all times.
4. Stay out of the woods.

Some speakers at campfires are like male Wild Adirondack cows. A point here, a point there, and a lot of bull in between.

More Scout Lore

Why do bees select buddies before they go swimming?
They like to Bee Pre-paired.

What do you call an ant that helps the patrol leader?
An assist ant patrol leader.

Why was the baby bear wearing blue?
He was a Cub Scout.

What do you get if you cross an elephant with a Boy Scout?
An elephant that helps old ladies cross the street.

What happened when 500 hares got loose at Scout camp?
The troop had to comb the area.

What should you do if you swallow a flashlight?
Spit it out and be delighted.

How many Scouts can you fit in an empty dining hall?
One, then it is no longer empty.

What do you get when you cross a monster and a Boy Scout?
A creature that scares old ladies across the street.

Why did the Scoutmaster put wheels on his rocking chair?
He wanted to rock and roll.

Why shouldn't you place a Scout camp near a chicken farm?
*You wouldn't want the campers to hear any fowl
language.*

Did you hear about the dizzy Boy Scout?
He spent the whole day doing good turns.

What does Smokey the Bear put in his backpack before a long hike?
Simply the bear essentials

What kind of shoes does a bear where at Scout Camp?
None, it goes bear foot.

The Animals at Camp

What did the deer say when they saw the Ranger coming over the hill?
Here comes the Ranger coming over the hill.

What did the deer say when he saw the Ranger coming over the hill wearing sunglasses?
Nothing, they didn't recognize him.

How can you keep a fish from smelling?
Cut off its nose.

Why isn't a skunk's nose 12 inches long?
Because then it would be a foot.

How can you revive a rodent that falls into a lake?
Mouse to Mouse resuscitation.

Why do mice have fur?
Otherwise they would be a little bare.

What kind of bank account does a mouse have?
A Swiss account.

Where does a mouse go when its teeth hurt?
To a rodent-ist.

How do mice find there way to new places?
With a road-ent map.

What insect is known to say grace before its meals?
A praying mantis.

Why do the bees at the soccer field hum?
They don't know the words.

What did the duck say when he bought lipstick?
Put it on my bill.

What did the impatient stag say to his wife?
Hurry up deer

Why do bees have sticky hair?
Because they have honeycombs.

What do bees do with their honey?
They cell it.

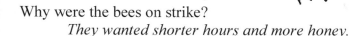

Why were the bees on strike?
They wanted shorter hours and more honey.

Why are crows so noisy after they've been stung?
Bee Caws.

What do you call a bee that speaks softly?
A mumble bee.

Why wouldn't the twin lobsters share their toys?
They were two shellfish.

How did the antelope and deer burn themselves?
Trying to make themselves at home on the range.

Why did the crow look for a telephone?
He wanted to make a long distance caw.

When birds fly in formation, why is one side of the V longer than the other?
Because one side has more birds in it.

What has a yellow stomach and sucks sap from trees?
A yellow bellied sap sucker.

What is a yellow bellied sap sucker after he is four days old?
5 days old.

What do you call a bee born in May?
A maybe.

What did the beaver say to the tree?
It was nice gnawing you.

Why do seagulls fly over the sea?
Because if they flew over the bay they would be bagels.

How much birdseed should you get for a buck?
None. Deer don't eat birdseed.

What animals can jump higher than the tallest tree at camp? *All animals. Trees can't jump.*

What animal is the best at Math?
Rabbits - they multiple very rapidly.

How do snakes call each other?
Poison to poison.

What is black and white and goes around and around?
A skunk in a revolving door.

In an outdoor Chapel, where does a skunk sit?
In a pew.

How do you stop a mouse from squeaking?
With a little motor oil.

Why was the mother owl worried about her son?
Because he didn't give a hoot about anything.

What is the last hair on a skunk's tail called?
A skunk hair.

What animal eats with its tail?
All animals. None of them can remove their tail to eat.

Why do ducks have webbed feet?
To stamp out forest fires.

Why do elephants have flat feet?
To stamp out burning ducks.

What's grey and stamps out forest fires?
Smokey the elephant.

Can skunks have babies?
No, they can only have skunks.

How come only small toads can sit under toadstools?
Because there isn't mushroom.

What does a skunk do when it gets mad?
It raises a stink.

How do you stop a snake from striking?
Pay it decent wages.

Why do rats have long tails?
Because they can't remember short stories.

What goes da-dot-croak, dot-dot-croak, da-da-dot croak?
A morse toad.

What should you do if you have 44 frogs on your back windshield?
Turn on the rear window defrogger.

What do you say to a hitchhiking frog?
Hop in.

The Camp Ranger's Riddles

Don't be stumped by the camp ranger.

How long will a seven day clock run without winding?
> *It won't run at all without winding.*

What happened to the skydiver whose parachute didn't open?
> *He jumped to a conclusion.*

What do you say when the Statue of Liberty sneezes?
> *God Bless America.*

Where were the first french fries made?
> *In Grease.*

What do people in Canada call little black cats?
> *Kittens.*

What happened when a ship carrying red paint collided with a ship carrying purple paint?
> *Both crews were marooned.*

What's the best way to get rid of evil spirits?
> *Exorcise a lot.*

How many apples grow on a tree?
> *All of them.*

Why do some people press the elevator button with their thumb and other people press it with their forefinger?
> *To signal for the elevator.*

What happened to the thief that stole a calendar?
> *He got 12 months.*

How do you make soup golden?
> *Just add 24 carrots.*

What happened to the cat that ate the ball of yarn?
> *It had mittens.*

What small blood sucking insect lives on the moon?
A lunatic.

What's the funniest animal in the world?
A stand up chameleon.

If there were 10 cats on a xerox machine and one jumped off how many would be left?
None - they were all copycats.

What do you call a cloistered priest eating potato chips?
A chip monk.

What do liars do when they die?
Lie still.

Do you say 6 plus 7 is eleven or 6 plus 7 are 11?
Neither, you say 6 plus 7 equals 13.

What is 5Q + 5Q?
When someone responds 10Q - say your welcome.

Who won the race between the cheetah and the gazelle?
The gazelle won because cheetahs never win.

What do Alexander the Great and Smokey the Bear have in common?
The same middle name.

Where can you go that it is so quiet you can hear a pin drop?
A bowling alley.

What do you call a person who is born in Russia, raised in China, moves to America and dies in Winsted, CT?
Dead.

Hermit the Frog

What do you get when you cross a frog and a male Wild Adirondack Cow?
> *A Bull Frog.*

What is Hermit the Frog's favorite flower?
> *A crocus.*

Who is green and lives alone in the woods?
> *Hermit the Frog.*

What famous Pole is related to Hermit the Frog?
> *Tad Pole.*

What does Hermit the Frog drink?
> *Croak-a-cola.*

What happened to Hermit the Frog when he sat in the no parking area?
> *He got toad away.*

How did Hermit the Frog die?
> *He croaked.*

Why couldn't Hermit the Frog speak?
> *He had a person in his throat.*

What did Hermit the Frog become when he broke his leg?
> *Unhoppy.*

Where does Hermit the Frog hang his jacket?
In the croak room.

What kind of shoes does Hermit the Frog like?
Open toad shoes.

What is Hermit the Frog's favorite game?
Croquet.

What game does his Scottish cousin like?
Hop Scotch.

Why is Hermit the Frog happy?
He gets to eat what bugs him.

Why did Hermit the Frog yell at the waiter?
There was no fly in his soup.

How does Hermit the Frog start his car when it won't turn over?
Jump start.

What did Hermit the Frog eat with his hamburger when he was in Paris?
French Flies.

What's evergreen, grows in the spring, and hops around?
A tree frog.

Joe Scout

What happened when Joe Scout ran behind the Scoutmaster's car?
He got exhausted.

What happened when Joe Scout wandered into the street looking for the traffic jam?
A big truck came by and gave him a jar.

When Joe Scout's sister fell in a well why didn't he help her?
Because he couldn't be a brother and assist her at the same time.

What did Joe Scout catch when he went ice fishing?
A cold.

How did Joe Scout clean the mouthpiece on his tuba?
With a tuba toothpaste.

Why does Joe Scout sleep on top of his electric blanket?
He heard heat rises.

Why did Joe Scout paint a red cross on his canteen before hiking across the desert?
He thought he should have a thirst aid kit.

Why couldn't Joe Scout blow up his old car?
He kept burning himself on the exhaust pipe.

Why did Joe Scout bring a stone into the bakery?
He wanted to rock and roll.

Why did Joe Scout take all his clothes off at the laundromat?
The sign said remove clothes when washer stops.

Why does Joe Scout write TGIF on all his shoes?
To remind him toes go in first.

Why did Joe Scout stand next to the bank vault?
He wanted to be on the safe side.

Why did Joe Scout go into the dressing room?
He heard he would come out a changed man.

Why did Joe Scout use nails for bait when he went fishing?
He was hoping to catch hammerhead sharks.

Why did Joe Scout order an egg salad sandwich and a chicken salad sandwich for lunch?
He wanted to see which came first.

Why did Joe Scout stuff his sausages with pork on one side and corn on the other?
He heard it was hard to make both ends meat.

How come Joe Scout had trouble trying to blow up a balloon?
He wasn't using enough dynamite.

Why was Joe Scout convinced his watch was running fast?
Because it took him an hour to make minute rice.

Why did Joe Scout put his head to the grindstone?
He wanted to sharpen his wit.

Why did Joe Scout give his mother an X-ray of his heart?
He wanted to show her that his heart was in the right place.

Why did Joe Scout bring a raisin to the movies?
He couldn't find a date.

Why did Joe Scout hold a piece of bread in the air?
He wanted to propose a toast.

What happened when Joe Scout swallowed some uranium?
He got atomic ache.

What did Joe Scout do when he was being chased in a circle by 42 horses?
He got off the merry-go-round.

How did Joe Scout get sand in his shoes while tree climbing?
He was climbing Beech trees.

When Joe Scout made a movie - why did he call it broken leg?
Because it had a big cast.

Why did Joe Scout eat under the lamppost?
He wanted to have a light lunch.

Why does Joe Scout need his whole patrol to help him make scrambled eggs?
One Scout needs to hold the pan while the others shake the stove.

Why did Joe Scout throw the clock out the window?
He wanted to see time fly.

Why did Joe Scout sleep under the oil tank?
He wanted to get up oily in the morning.

Why was Joe Scout so tired on April fool's day?
He just had a March of 31 days.

Why did Joe Scout eat yeast and polish?
He wanted to rise and shine.

What happened to Joe Scout after he broke the law of gravity?
He got a suspended sentence.

Why was Joe Scout limping?
He strained himself walking through the screen door.

Why did Joe Scout buy a set of tools?
Because everyone kept telling him he had a screw loose.

Why was Joe Scout glad he wasn't born in Germany?
Because he can't speak German.

Why does Joe Scout carry a compass?
So he'll know whether he's coming or going.

What happened when Joe Scout threw himself on the floor?
He missed.

Why did Joe Scout stand on a ladder to sing the camp song?
He wanted to reach the high notes.

Why did Joe Scout stare at the orange juice container?
It said concentrate on it.

Why did Joe Scout put an ice-pack in his father's sleeping bag?
He wanted to have a cold pop.

Why did Joe Scout sell his alarm clock?
It kept going off when he was asleep.

Why did Joe Scout pour pancake batter on his electric blanket?
He wanted breakfast in bed.

Why did Joe Scout spray bug spray on his watch?
He wanted to get rid of the ticks.

What did Joe Scout act like a nut?
He wanted to catch a squirrel.

Why did Joe Scout take his pocket knife and a loaf of bread into the street?
He heard there was a traffic jam.

Why did Joe Scout lock his mother's sister out of the cabin during a snowstorm?
He wanted to make anti-freeze.

Why did Joe Scout put a sugar cube under his pillow?
He wanted to have sweet dreams.

Why did Joe Scout take hay into his tent at bedtime?
He wanted to feed his nightmares.

Why did Joe Scout empty his canteen?
He wanted to see a waterfall.

Why did Joe Scout sit on his watch?
He wanted to be on time for the meeting.

Why did Joe Scout tiptoe past his tent?
He didn't want to wake up the sleeping bags.

How did Joe Scout break his leg raking leaves?
He fell out of the tree.

Why did Joe Scout throw a stick of butter in the air?
He wanted to see a butterfly.

What did Joe Scout take out his pocketknife and slice his toe?
He was running late and wanted to make a shortcut.

What did Joe Scout say when he wore a hole through his socks?
Darn them.

Why did Joe Scout cut a hole in his umbrella?
He wanted to see when the rain stopped.

Why was Joe Scout glad he wasn't an eagle?
He couldn't fly.

Why did Joe Scout put his head on the piano?
He wanted to play by ear.

Why did Joe Scout tie a flashlight to his bed?
Because he was a light sleeper.

Why did Joe Scout put his radio in the freezer?
He wanted to hear cool music.

Why did Joe Scout wear loud colorful socks?
He wanted to keep his feet from falling asleep.

What did Joe Scout call his pet zebra?
Spot.

What did Joe Scout call his black horse?
Night Mare.

Why did Joe Scout cut a hole in the carpet?
He wanted to see the floor show.

Why did Joe Scout eat a dollar?
It was his lunch money.

Why did Joe Scout give up waterskiing?
He couldn't find a lake with a hill in it.

Why did Joe Scout give cough syrup to the pony?
Someone told him the pony was a little horse.

Why did Joe Scout pitch his tent on the oven?
So he could have a home on the range.

Why did Joe Scout wear a wet T-shirt to bed?
The label said, "Wash and wear."

Why did Joe Scout bury the car battery?
Because it was dead.

Where was Joe Scout when the lights went out?
In the dark.

Why did Joe Scout take a ruler to bed?
He wanted to see how long he would sleep.

Why did Joe Scout reach for a bar of soap when his canoe overturned?
He thought he would wash up on shore.

Joe Beagle Scout

The exciting adventures of Joe Scout's dog, Joe Beagle Scout.

How did Joe Scout stop his dog, Joe Beagle, from barking in the back seat of his car?
> *He had Joe Beagle sit in the front.*

What happened when Joe Beagle chewed on a dictionary?
> *Joe Scout had to take the words right out of his mouth.*

What did Joe Beagle say when he sat on a piece of sandpaper?
> *Ruff-ruff.*

Why did Joe Beagle run in circles?
> *He was winding himself so that he could become a watchdog.*

Why did Joe Beagle sit on the campfire?
> *He wanted to be a hot dog.*

What is Joe Beagle's favorite drink?
> *Pupsi Cola.*

What happened to Joe Beagle after he ate garlic for a month?
> *His bark became worse than his bite.*

What goes Krab, ffur, krab, ffur?
> *Joe beagle walking backwards.*

Why did Joe Beagle have to pay a fine?
> *He got a barking ticket.*

Is Joe Beagle a good watch dog?
> *Absolutely! If you hear a noise in the middle of the night and you wake him up, he'll bark like crazy.*

What does Joe Beagle do that Joe Scout steps into?
> *Pants.*

Trader Jack's Riddles

Why did the workers at the U.S. mint go on strike?
They wanted to make less money.

What do you get when you cross a lemon with a cat?
A sour puss.

If people in America drove only white cars, what would our country be?
A white car-nation.

What happened to the man who fell into the lens grinding machine?
He made a spectacle of himself.

What happened to the dentist who married a manicurist?
They fought tooth and nail.

What was the highest mountain before Mount Everest was discovered?
Mount Everest.

Did you hear about the new restaurant on the moon?
The food is great but there's no atmosphere.

What school did Sherlock Holmes graduate from?
Elementary, my dear Watson.

How do you spell blind pig?
B-L-N-D P-G. A blind pig doesn't have any eyes.

What lies at the bottom of the ocean and quivers?
A nervous wreck.

Why didn't the cannibal eat the clown?
He tasted funny.

What do you call a deer with no eyes?
No eye deer   (no idea).

What do you call a deer with no eyes and no legs?
Still, no eye deer.

Indians in Camp

What kind of Indian is always going to court?
A Sioux Indian.

Why did the Indian wear feathers in his hair?
To keep his wig warm.

What do the Indians call a twisted path through their corn fields?
A maize.

What three letters does Chief Sequassen use to signify his heritage?
N D N.

What did they call Chief Sequassen's single daughter when she got in trouble?
Mischief.

What did Chief Sequassen call the ranger when he got his head caught in a bucket?
Pail face.

What's an Indian forum?
Two-um plus two-um.

Did the local Indians hunt bear?
Not when it was cold out.

What did the local Indians call 5 frogs stacked on top of each other?
A toad-em pole.

An American Indian, a Boy Scout, and a Rabbi enter a hotel with no vacancies. Why did the Indian get a room?
Indians have reservations.

What type of shoes do Indians wear during rain dances?
Pumps.

The Trading Post

Scout: How much do used batteries cost?
Trader Jack: Nothing they're free of charge.

Scout: Excuse me, but do you have a watermelon patch at the trading post?
Trader Jack: Why, is your watermelon leaking?

Scout: Do you carry tomato paste?
Trader Jack: Why do you have a broken tomato?

Scout: Toss me a box of that writing paper.
Trader Jack: I can't toss it if it's stationary.

Trader Jack: I hear Jester got a job at The Good Revolving Door Company.
Scout: Really?
Trader Jack: Yeah, I guess he helps make sure a lot of people do a good turn daily.

Trader Jack: This is genuine Indian pottery.
Scout: But it says on the bottom made in Cleveland.
Trader Jack: Well haven't you ever heard of the Cleveland Indians?

Little Old Lady: Young man, I'd like to go to the trading post. Will you help me across the street?
Scout: Yes, but it would be easier if I helped you right here.
Little Old Lady: No, what I mean is, would you see me across the street?
Scout: Gee, I'm not sure. I'll run across and have a look.

Joe Scout: Hey, look! I bought this giant pack of cards at the trading post.
The Ranger: Big Deal.

Scout versus Scoutmaster

Scoutmaster: Each of you needs to eat all of your vegetables. There are thousands of starving children who would love to have them.

Scout: Name two.

Scoutmaster: Why do you always have to answer my questions with another question?

Scout: Why not?

Scout: If I'm good throughout the entire camping trip, will you give me a dollar?

Scoutmaster: Absolutely not! When I was your age I was good for nothing.

Scout: What causes the holes in those boards?

Scoutmaster: Those are knot holes.

Scout: If they're not holes, what are they?

Scoutmaster: Do any of you boys know who homer was?

Scout: Yeah, he was the guy Babe Ruth made famous.

Scoutmaster: Can you telephone from a submarine?

Scout: Of course, everyone can tell a phone from a submarine.

Scoutmaster: What made you go out on that unsafe ice and risk your life to save your friend?

Scout: I had to do it; he was wearing my skates.

Scoutmaster: Why are you guys returning so late from the orienteering course?

Scout: We were following this Tates compass, but it kept sending us in circles.

Scoutmaster: You idiots. Don't you know he who has a Tates is lost!

Scout: I'm too tired to wash the dishes.
Scoutmaster: Nonsense, a little hard work never killed anyone.
Scout: Then why should I run the risk of being the first?

Scoutmaster: Why are you carrying only one log for the campfire, when all the other Scouts have their hands completely full?
Scout: I guess the other Scouts are too lazy to make more than one trip.

Scoutmaster: The only way to acquire a new skill is to start at the bottom.
Scout: But I want to learn to swim.

Scoutmaster: When I was young my parents told me if I made ugly faces my face would stay that way forever.
Scout: Well, you can't say you weren't warned.

Scout: At summer camp we slept in 20 foot long beds.
Scoutmaster: That sounds like a lot of bunk to me.

Scoutmaster: Can someone tell me anything about soldiers from the Revolutionary War?
Scout: They're all dead.

Scoutmaster: To complete your bird study merit badge you must name these three birds.
Scout: This is easy. I'll name them Harold, Irving and Polly.

Scoutmaster: How did you get that black eye?
Scout: Sir, I was hit by a guided muscle with a knucklear warhead!

Scoutmaster: I lost my toupee this morning.
Scout: I think we should comb the area.

Jester and Joe Scout

Jester: Did I ever tell you about the time I came face to face with a mountain lion?

Joe Scout: No. What happened?

Jester: Well, I was totally unarmed. I stood my ground but he kept inching closer and closer toward me.

Joe Scout: What did you do?

Jester: Finally, I moved on to the next cage.

Jester: This match won't light.

Joe Scout: What's the matter with it?

Jester: I don't know, it worked a couple of minutes ago.

Jester: What's the difference between an elephant and a matterboy?

Joe Scout: What's a matterboy?

Jester: Nothing. What's a matter with you?

Jester: Hey, Joe, want to work on a new merit badge?

Joe Scout: Sure, what are the requirements?

Jester: It's easy. All you need to do is hike 5 miles through poison ivy.

Joe Scout: What merit badge is that?

Jester: Itch-hiking.

Jester: Did you hear about the latest sport to be having labor problems?

Joe Scout: No.

Jester: It seems professional bowlers have been talking strike.

Joe Scout: My Scout uniform is always wrinkled, and my mom and I always fight about it.

Jester: I think you two should sit down and iron things out.

Jester: Did you hear the joke about the boy who fell on a bag of potato chips?

Joe Scout: No.

Jester: It's crummy.

Joe Scout: Mary, would you like to go out with me Saturday night?
Mary: I'm not really looking to get involved with one particular guy right now, Joe.
Joe Scout: Well lucky for you, I'm not known for being particular.

Joe Scout: My cabin on the boat was nice, but that washing machine on the wall was terrible?
Jester: That was no washing machine. That was the port hole.
Joe Scout: Well no wonder I didn't get any of my clothes back.

Jester: If I can prove that food is the mother of invention will you give me $10.00?
Joe Scout: OK.
Jester: Well food is a necessity, and an airplane is an invention and everyone knows that necessity is the mother of invention. Cough up the 10 bucks.

Jester: Do you want to see something swell?
Joe Scout: Sure.
Jester: Hit your head with a baseball bat.

Joe Scout: I'm always breaking into song.
Jester: You wouldn't have to if you could find the right key.

Jester: Joe, how much after midnight is it?
Joe Scout: I don't know. My watch only goes up to twelve.

Jester: How can you tell a dogwood tree apart from other trees?
Joe Scout: How?
Jester: By its bark.

More With Joe Beagle Scout

Joe Beagle Scout

Jester: Do you have a license for your dog, Joe Beagle?
Joe Scout: No, he's not old enough to drive.

Joe Scout: Jester, I'm so worried. I lost my dog.
Jester: Why don't you put an ad in the paper?
Joe Scout: It wouldn't help. My dog can't read.

Joe Scout: My dog is very smart.
Jester: Joe Beagle is absolutely the dumbest dog I've ever seen.
Joe Scout: That's not true. Joe Beagle is good at math.
Jester: Really?
Joe Scout: Absolutely. I once asked him how much is 10 minus 10. Sure enough, Joe Beagle said nothing.
Jester: Why is your dog running around in a circle like that?
Joe Scout: He thinks he's a watchdog, and he's winding himself.

Joe Scout: You look tired.
Jester: I ought to be. I was up all night chasing the dog in my pajamas.
Joe Scout: What was the dog doing in your pajamas?

Joe Scout: Do you like my dog? It's a very rare breed. Part beagle and part bull. He cost me over two thousand dollars.
Jester: Really? Which part is bull?
Joe Scout: The part about the two thousand dollars.

Jester: We have a new dog too.
Joe Scout: What's he like?
Jester: Whatever we feed him.

Jester: Can you believe it. My dog doesn't even have a nose.
Joe Scout: How does he smell?
Jester: Terrible.

Jester: Joe, your dog has been chasing a man on a bicycle.
Joe Scout: That's silly, my dog doesn't know how to ride a bike.

Joe Scout: Why does Joe Beagle wag his tail?
Jester: Because no one else will wag it for him.

Joe Scout: Why is your dog staring at me while I'm eating?
Jester: He gets like that whenever someone eats from his plate.

Joe Scout: My dog's neck is always hanging down. I'm going to take him to the vet.
Jester: Neck's weak?
Joe Scout: No, tomorrow.

Teacher: Joe, your short story entitled "My Dog" reads exactly the same as your brother's.
Joe Scout: It's the same dog, sir.

Jester: Did you know that there's a star called the dog star?
Joe Scout: Are you Sirius?

More with Jester and Joe Scout

Joe Scout:	Do you want to hear me sing the camp song?
Jester:	Only if it's solo.
Joe Scout:	What do you mean?
Jester:	Only if it's so low I can't hear it.

Jester:	Jimmy says he's related to you and he can prove it.
Joe Scout:	Jimmy is an idiot.
Jester:	That part is probably just a coincidence.

Jester:	Did you hear about my pinewood derby car?
Joe Scout:	No.
Jester:	It was a wooden car with wooden wheels and a wooden engine. The only problem I had was it wooden go.

Jester:	Lend me 50 cents.
Joe Scout:	I only have forty.
Jester:	In that case, give me 40. You can owe me a dime.

Joe Scout:	I'd like to go on a date with a girl who's the exact opposite of me.
Jester:	No problem Joe, there are a lot of bright girls around.

Joe Scout:	Hey Jester, what are you doing?
Jester:	Writing a letter to my little sister.
Joe Scout:	How come you're writing it so slowly?
Jester:	Because she can't read very fast.

Jester:	Hey Joe, how old would a person be who was born in 1950?
Joe Scout:	Man or woman?

Jester:	Joe, I heard you singing this morning.
Joe Scout:	Yeah, I was just killing time.
Jester:	Looks like you had an effective weapon.

Jester:	Do you know how many sheep it takes to make a sweater?
Joe Scout:	I didn't even know they could knit.

Jester:	Joe, you hammer nails like lightning.
Joe Scout:	You mean I'm fast?
Jester:	No, I mean you never strike the same place twice.

Jester:	You really remind me of a flower.
Joe Scout:	Why's that?
Jester:	Because you're a blooming idiot.

Jester:	Do you have holes in your underwear?
Joe Scout:	No.
Jester:	Then how do you put your feet through?

Jester:	The newspaper says that the police want a man for holding up the trading post.
Joe Scout:	How long do you have to hold it for?
Jester:	No stupid, they want a man for robbing the trading post.
Joe Scout:	Well how much does the job pay?

Joe Scout:	Jester, I'm going to sing for you.
Jester:	Sing tenor.
Joe Scout:	Tenor?
Jester:	Ten or eleven miles from here.

Jester:	What is the first letter in yellow?
Joe Scout:	Y.
Jester:	Because I want to know.

Joe Scout:	Did you meet your sister at the train station?
Jester:	No, I've known her for years.

Jester:	I bet you I can tell you the score of the game before it starts.
Joe Scout:	No way.
Jester:	Nothing to nothing.

Jester:	If you can guess how many candy bars I have I'll give you both of them.
Joe Scout:	Hmmmm.....I'll say three.

Jester:	I earned my cooking merit badge by making an upside down cake on an open campfire.
Joe Scout:	How'd it turn out?
Jester:	Actually, it was a complete flop.

Joe Scout:	I've eaten beef all my life and now I'm strong as a bull.
Jester:	That's funny, I've eaten fish all my life and I can't swim a stroke.

Joe Scout:	The two things I cook best are meatloaf and upside down cake.
Jester:	Which one is this?

Joe Scout:	A bee stung me!!!
Jester:	Try putting some ointment on it.
Joe Scout:	But the bee's probably miles away by now.

Jester:	I tied a piece of yellow string around my finger to keep lions away while we're at camp.
Joe Scout:	There are no lions here.
Jester:	Good, the string seems to be working.

Jester:	Don't open my trunk. It contains a 10 foot snake.
Joe Scout:	You can't fool me. Even I know snakes don't have 10 feet.

Joe Scout:	I crashed my bicycle. I went out for a ride, and I hit a cow.
Jester:	A jersey cow?
Joe Scout:	I don't know. I didn't see the license plate.

Learn From The Ranger

The Ranger: That bird over there is known as a gulp.
Joe Scout: A gulp? I never heard of that before.
The Ranger: Oh, it's very much like a swallow only bigger.

The Ranger: That there is a very unusual bird known as an invisible cockle.
Joe Scout: What's so unusual about an invisible cockle?
The Ranger: Oh, you don't see one every day.

The Ranger: You are letting too much updock grow on your arms Joe.
Joe Scout: What's updock?
The Ranger: Not much you wrascally rabbit.

Joe Scout: Is it all right if we climb that flagpole?
The Ranger: It's O.K., but if you break your leg, don't come running to me.

The Ranger: Do you want a saddle with or without a horn?
Joe Scout: Without. You don't get much traffic here.

Joe Scout: Ranger, I understand that you earned the Medal of Honor.
The Ranger: Yes that's true. I once saved the lives of the entire camp.
Joe Scout: That's incredible. How did you do it?
The Ranger: I fired the cook.

The Ranger: The eagle patrol just had a real hair raising experience.
Joe Scout: Really?
The Ranger: They just got back from visiting a rabbit farm.

The Ranger: (at the rifle range): Ready. Aim. Fire at will.
Joe Scout: Which one is Will?

Joe Scout: I think we're lost. I thought you said you were the best guide in camp?

The Ranger: I am, but we're not in camp any more.

The Ranger: This is a dogwood tree.

Joe Scout: How can you tell?

The Ranger: By its bark.

The Ranger: Leave Joe Scout alone.

Jester: How come?

The Ranger: He's recovering from an unusual incident.

Jester: What happened?

Ranger: A thought struck him.

The Ranger: Did you do your good deed for the day?

Joe Scout: Absolutely, the Scouts in my patrol and I helped an old lady across the street.

The Ranger: How come it took four of you to help someone cross the street?

Joe Scout: She didn't want to cross.

The Ranger: Joe, what is the outer part of a sycamore tree called?

Jester: I don't know.

The Ranger: Bark, Joe. Bark?

Jester: O.K. Woof, woof.

The Ranger: What looks like a Holstein, has sharp teeth and is full of cement?

Joe Scout: I give up.

The Ranger: A Wild Adirondack Cow.

Joe Scout: But what about the part about cement?

The Ranger: I just threw that in to make it hard.

Joe Scout: My tentmate thinks he's a refrigerator.

The Ranger: Don't let it bother you.

Joe Scout: I can't help it. He's sleeping with his mouth open and the light is keeping me awake.

Order your Scout Fun Books today!

Scout Riddles

Superior Campfires

The Scout Puzzle & Activity Book

Scout Skits

Scout Jokes

Scoutmaster's Minutes

Scoutmaster's Minutes II

More Scout Skits

Along the Scouting Trail

Campfire Tales

Run-ons and Even More Scout Skits

Scout Games

For an updated list of available books along with current pricing visit: *scoutfunbooks.webs.com*
or find our books on Amazon!

Books are also available on a wholesale basis to qualified Scout Troops, Council Shops, trading posts in quantities of 50 or more. Contact us by email at BoyScoutBooks@aol.com.

Made in America

cilantro secrets

Rio Nuevo Publishers®
P.O. Box 5250, Tucson, Arizona 85703-0250
(520) 623-9558, www.rionuevo.com

Text and photography © 2006 by Rio Nuevo Publishers. Food styling
by Tracy Vega. Many thanks to AJ's Fine Foods and to Jeannine Brookshire for
providing beautiful settings and amenities for the photo shoots for this book.

Photography credits as follows:
W. Ross Humphreys: front cover, pages 2-3, 4 (right), 17, 18, 23, 39, 40, 43, 65
Robin Stancliff: pages 4 (left), 5, 15, 28, 33, 34, 49, 52, 62, 71
Katy Parks Wilson: back cover, pages 11, 31, 77

Library of Congress Cataloging-in-Publication Data
Doland, Gwyneth.
  Cilantro secrets / Gwyneth Doland.
    p. cm. — (Cook west series)
Includes index.
ISBN-13: 978-1-887896-92-4 (pbk.)
ISBN-10: 1-887896-92-9 (pbk.)
1. Cookery (Coriander) 2. Cookery, American—Southwestern style.
I. Title. II. Series.
TX819.C65D65 2006
641.6'57—dc22

                                    2005037700

Design: Karen Schober, Seattle, Washington.

Printed in Korea.

10 9 8 7 6 5 4 3 2 1

cilantro
secrets

GWYNETH DOLAND

RIO NUEVO PUBLISHERS
TUCSON, ARIZONA

contents

xxxxxx

I am living proof that cilantro does not have to be a love-it-or-hate-it ingredient. People do have extremely strong opinions about this herb (unlike its close relative, parsley), and many people either absolutely adore the pungent, citrusy flavor of its bright green leaves—or they can't stand the sight of it. But I know for sure that tastes can change.

As a child, I persistently removed every trace of cilantro from bowls of grilled pork and rice vermicelli at our favorite Vietnamese restaurant. Back then, I thought cilantro smelled like dirty socks and firmly believed I would hate it forever. Today, after years of exposure, I think it smells fresh and clean. I've gone from hating cilantro to loving this herb, which is used every day by millions of cooks around the world.

Cilantro (*Coriandrum sativum*) is a native of the Mediterranean and is the same plant that gives us the spice coriander, which comes from its seeds. It is an annual herb of the *Umbelliferae* family, a group that includes other delicate, leafy-topped plants such as dill, chervil, fennel, parsley, carrots, and parsnips. The whole plant, from leaves to stems, seeds, and root, is edible and is generally referred to as coriander. The name coriander comes from the Greek word *corys*, meaning "bedbug," and the suffix *ander* meaning "resembling," because the ancient Greeks thought it smelled like stinky bugs. In the United States and many Latin American countries, the leaves are referred to as cilantro, a word borrowed from Spanish. This can be confusing, because the stem and seeds taste nothing alike and cannot be substituted for one another.

Coriander seeds have long been a part of the world's spice cabinet. Exported today primarily from Morocco and Romania, the small, ridged, brown seeds are combined with other spices to make Indian curry powder and *garam masala*. They are also used to flavor English gin, German sausages, Middle

Eastern pastries, Belgian beers, and American cigarettes. Coriander root is a popular ingredient in Thai cooking and is found in some Chinese dishes, but it is rarely used in other cuisines and not often found in American markets. (If you grow your own cilantro you can try cooking coriander root. Look for a recipe in your favorite Thai cookbook.)

Both cilantro and coriander have a long history of culinary use in many cultures. Coriander seeds discovered in a cave in Israel are believed to be more than 8,000 years old, and cilantro leaves were mentioned in Sanskrit texts that date back nearly 7,000 years. An Egyptian papyrus written around 1552 B.C. mentions cilantro, and a large cache of coriander seed was found in King Tut's tomb. The Bible even mentions the spice in Exodus 16:31: "And the house of Israel called the name there of Manna: and it was like coriander seed, but white; and the taste of it was like wafers made with honey." Cilantro was one of the plants that grew in the famed hanging gardens of Babylon and was used by ancient Hebrews as the symbolic bitter herb for the Passover seder. It was even believed to have aphrodisiac qualities—a story in *The Arabian Nights* recounts how a childless merchant finally became a father after drinking a potion made from the plant.

In America, cilantro could be found in the earliest gardens planted by European settlers. It had been brought to the New World in the early sixteenth century and quickly spread. By 1598 it was cultivated in what is now New Mexico, and in 1670 it was growing in what would become Massachusetts. Although the popularity of cilantro may have lain dormant for several hundred years in the Northeast, it never waned in the Southwest, where it remains an ever-present ingredient and garnish. In fact, cilantro is pervasive throughout Latin American cuisines, and as Americans' consumption of salsa and enchiladas (not to mention curry and couscous) has risen over the past few decades, so has our interest in ingredients like cilantro.

Cilantro lends itself well to cool and refreshing foods similar to those found in the hot-weather regions where it is popular. Sometimes called Chinese parsley, cilantro is to be found in every cuisine of Asia (with the notable exception of Japanese), although in American restaurants it is perhaps most prominent in Thai and Vietnamese dishes. Cilantro is also a vital ingredient in East Indian, Middle Eastern, and North African foods. The more you explore the foods of the world, the more you will find cilantro—not lurking, but *starring* in national dishes.

No matter in which corner of the globe you find cilantro, however, you'll rarely come across it in a form other than freshly snipped. Cilantro's thin, feathery leaves are too delicate to survive long cooking, so they're almost always added to finished dishes as a garnish. Drying deprives the hollow-stemmed stalks of nearly all of their pungency, which is why you'll rarely see cilantro sold in a spice jar.

Not to worry. You'll find cilantro in markets all year long. Look for bunches without any yellow leaves or signs of wilting. Carefully wash and dry the leaves and stems, then store the bunch, stem ends down, in a water glass in the refrigerator. Cover the whole thing loosely with a plastic bag and secure it with a rubber band. If you change the water every day, your cilantro will last well over a week. Just remember to snip off only as much as you plan to use immediately, as the leaves lose their pungency soon after being chopped.

If you already love cilantro, then these 50 recipes will give you that many more excuses to cook with this uniquely flavorful herb. (As a general rule, you can also try it in any dish that calls for parsley.) If you think you hate cilantro or you're still on the fence, let this book be your guide on a culinary journey that just might help you fall in love. Try some of these dishes, from the familiar pico de gallo to exotic squash blossom quesadillas, or from cornmeal crepes to Crying Tiger steaks, using just a little cilantro at first. You'll find your tolerance will turn to adoration and then addiction!

Salsas

Grilled Pineapple Chipotle Salsa

xxxxxx

Makes about 5 cups

1 fresh pineapple

1 red onion

Oil for the grill rack

2 cloves garlic, finely chopped

Juice of 1 lime

$1/4$ cup chopped cilantro leaves

Salt

Chipotle powder (see Sources, page 77)

This tropical salsa is great served with tortilla chips or ladled over shrimp tacos.

Preheat a gas or charcoal grill and make sure the grill rack is very clean.

Using a heavy knife, trim the top and bottom from the pineapple and quarter it. Cut the onion into ½-inch rings.

Lightly brush the grill rack with oil and grill the pineapple and onion pieces for a few minutes on each side, until slightly charred. Remove from the heat and allow to cool.

Trim the bumpy outer skin and tough core from the pineapple wedges. Chop the grilled fruit into bite-size pieces.

In a bowl, combine the pineapple, onion, garlic, lime juice, and cilantro. Add salt and chipotle powder to taste.

Charred Tomatillo Salsa

xxxxxx

Tomatillos look like small green tomatoes covered with thin, papery husks. Their citrusy, fruity flavor is an excellent match with cilantro. Use this salsa as a dip with chips or as a topping for grilled meat, or add it to mashed avocados for a quick guacamole.

Put the tomatillos into a heavy skillet set over medium-high heat and cook until softened. Allow them to char a little on each side, shaking the pan occasionally to redistribute them. Set aside. When they are cool enough to handle, remove the papery husks.

Over a gas flame, under a broiler, or on a grill, roast the chiles until dark and blistered. Place them in a bowl and cover with plastic wrap until cool enough to handle. Remove the stems, seeds, and charred skin.

In a blender or food processor, combine tomatillos, peeled chiles, onion, and garlic.

Add cilantro and salt to taste. If the salsa is very thick, add water until the desired consistency is reached, and reseason.

Makes about 2½ cups

1 pound tomatillos, washed and dried, husks left intact

2 New Mexico or Anaheim green chiles

1 small onion, roughly chopped

2 cloves garlic

1/3 cup finely chopped cilantro

Salt

Pico de Gallo

xxxxxx

Makes about 3 cups

1 pound tomatoes, chopped

1 small onion, chopped

1–2 jalapeños, seeded and finely chopped

1/3 cup chopped cilantro

Juice of 1 lime, or more, to taste

Salt

Pico de gallo, the most common salsa in Mexico, is quick and easy and goes well with almost anything. Use it to top eggs, steaks, and tacos, or simply serve it with tortilla chips.

In a bowl, combine the tomatoes, onion, jalapeños, and cilantro. Add lime juice and salt to taste. Allow the mixture to sit at room temperature for about 30 minutes to let the flavors fully develop.

Mango Habanero Salsa (pictured)

xxxxxx

Makes 3 cups

2 large mangos, peeled, seeded, and diced

1/2 cup chopped red onion

1/2 cup chopped cilantro leaves

Juice of 1 lime, more or less, to taste

Salt

1/2 habanero, finely chopped

The flavor of habanero chiles matches well with tropical fruit, and this salsa is great with grilled pork or seafood. Habanero chiles are very, very hot, and you should use gloves when handling them.

In a bowl, combine the mangos, onion, and cilantro. Add lime juice and salt to taste. Add habanero a little at a time, until the desired heat level is reached.

Fresh Corn Salsa

xxxxxx

Makes 3 cups

2 cups fresh corn kernels, cut from the cob (about 3 ears)

1/2 red bell pepper, diced

1/2 orange bell pepper, diced

1/4 cup sliced green onions

1/4 cup chopped cilantro leaves

Juice of 1 lime, or more, to taste

Salt and pepper

Don't make this unless you can get fresh summer corn; it won't be nearly as good made with frozen or canned corn. Use it as a topping for steaks or salmon, or as a garnish for summer soups. Feel free to add chiles if you like.

In a heavy skillet, cook the corn until the edges start to brown. Add a little water if the kernels dry out too much.

In a bowl, combine the cooked corn, red and orange bell peppers, green onions, and cilantro. Season with lime juice, salt, and pepper to taste.

Mexican Shrimp Cocktail

xxxxxx

Called vuelve la vida, *this is a common Mexican hangover remedy, but you don't need to wait until the morning after to enjoy it.*

Bring a large pot of water to a boil, add the salt and the shrimp, and cook until the shrimp are completely pink, about 2 minutes. Remove from heat, drain, and rinse in cold water. Remove the shells.

In a bowl, combine the ketchup, lime juice, avocado, jalapeño, garlic, cilantro, and green onions. Season with salt and pepper. Add a little water if the sauce seems too thick. Toss shrimp in sauce and serve chilled, in tall glasses.

Serves 4–6

1 teaspoon salt

1 $1/2$ pounds large shell-on shrimp

$1/2$ cup ketchup

$1/4$ cup lime juice

1 avocado, peeled and chopped

1 jalapeño, seeded and minced

1 clove garlic, minced

2 tablespoons finely chopped cilantro

2 green onions, sliced

Salt and freshly ground black pepper

Spicy Eggplant Dip with Wonton Chips

XXXXXX

1 large eggplant

1 tablespoon finely chopped garlic

1 tablespoon finely chopped gingerroot

1 teaspoon red chile flakes

3 tablespoons soy sauce

3 tablespoons brown sugar

1 teaspoon rice vinegar (see Sources, page 77)

1 tablespoon hot water

$1/2$ teaspoon sesame oil

2 tablespoons peanut oil

Additional peanut oil for frying wonton wrappers

20 wonton wrappers

$1/4$ cup finely chopped cilantro

This recipe is adapted from the Strange Flavor Eggplant that the late Barbara Tropp served at her San Francisco restaurant, the China Moon Café. When I worked at Albuquerque's Chef du Jour, we served it with fried wonton skins, but you can also spread it on crusty bread or serve it as a side dish. Wonton wrappers can be found in the produce department at grocery stores, near bricks of tofu.

Preheat the oven to 475 degrees F. Slice the eggplant in half, place cut side down on a baking sheet, and prick each half several times with a fork. Bake until tender, about 20 minutes.

Meanwhile, in a small bowl, combine the garlic, gingerroot, and chile flakes. In another small bowl, stir together the soy sauce, brown sugar, rice vinegar, hot water, and sesame oil.

Remove the eggplant from the oven. When cool enough to handle, peel the eggplant halves, chop the pulp, and puree in a food processor until smooth.

Add the 2 tablespoons of peanut oil to a heavy skillet or wok over medium-high heat. Add the garlic mixture and fry about 15 seconds. Add the soy sauce mixture and fry until it simmers. Add the eggplant and stir until heated through. Remove from heat and allow to cool.

Pour additional peanut oil into a heavy skillet or wok to a depth of 1½ inches and heat until a piece of wonton wrapper sizzles when dropped in the oil. Cut the wonton wrappers in half diagonally and fry a few at a time, until all are crispy and brown. Drain on paper towels.

Stir the cilantro into the eggplant dip and serve with the prepared crispy wonton chips.

Garlicky Bruschetta
xxxxxx

Rubbing grilled bread with cloves of garlic gives the bread a mild garlic flavor. Rub more for a stronger flavor, or very lightly for just a hint of garlic.

Serves 4–6

1 long baguette of crusty French bread

2–4 cloves garlic

$\frac{1}{2}$ pound fresh mozzarella

3 medium tomatoes

Salt and freshly ground black pepper

$\frac{1}{4}$ cup cilantro pesto

$\frac{1}{2}$ cup cilantro sprigs

Preheat the oven to 350 degrees F.

Slice the baguette into 12 pieces. Arrange the slices on a cookie sheet and bake for 5 minutes, then turn them over, and bake 5 more minutes.

Rub the garlic cloves over the surface of the toasted bread. Top the bread with slices of fresh mozzarella and tomatoes. Sprinkle with salt and pepper and finish each with a dollop of Cilantro Pesto (see page 55) and a sprig of fresh cilantro.

Chunky Guacamole with Chicharrones

xxxxxx

Makes 2 cups

2 large, ripe avocados, pitted, peeled, and roughly chopped

1 small onion, finely chopped

2 cloves garlic, finely chopped

1–2 jalapeños, seeded and finely chopped

¼ cup finely chopped cilantro leaves

Juice of 1 lime, or to taste

Salt

Even if you think you'll hate it, try pairing this guacamole with chicharrones *(fried pork skins) instead of tortilla chips. It's great!*

In a bowl, combine the avocado, onion, garlic, jalapeño, cilantro, and about 2 teaspoons of the lime juice. Stir gently with a fork, but don't mash the mixture into a paste; it should be chunky.

Add more lime juice and salt to taste. If you don't plan to serve it right away, press a layer of plastic wrap into the entire surface of the guacamole and refrigerate.

Squash Blossom Quesadillas

xxxxxx

Serves 4–8

12 squash blossoms

Corn oil for frying

8 small flour tortillas

1 1/2 cups grated
asadero cheese

1/2 cup cilantro leaves

Salsa, for dipping

Pick squash blossoms from your over-producing squash plants, or look for them at farmers markets during the summer months. Asadero is a mild Mexican cheese, also known as Oaxaca or Chihuahua cheese, that melts like Monterey Jack. Serve these quesadillas with any of the salsas in this book (starting on page 12).

Carefully wash and dry the squash blossoms, checking for lurking insects, and remove the stamens. Tear each blossom into 2 or 3 pieces.

In a heavy skillet, heat about 1 tablespoon of oil over medium heat. Add 1 tortilla. When it begins to color, turn it over. Quickly sprinkle one half of the tortilla with some of the cheese, squash blossom pieces, and cilantro leaves.

Fold the other half of the tortilla over the filling and gently press it down. Cook for about 2 minutes, until the cheese has partially melted. Turn and cook for about 2 more minutes, until the cheese is fully melted.

Repeat with the remaining tortillas and serve immediately with salsa.

Thai-style Shrimp Ceviche

xxxxxx

Traditional ceviches do not involve cooking the fish or shrimp; they rely on the acidity of lime or other citrus juice to cure the seafood. Since it is possible (although not probable) for diners to get sick from eating raw shellfish, the shrimp in this dish are cooked before being marinated in lime juice.

In a deep bowl, combine lime juice, red pepper flakes, garlic, fish sauce, cilantro, and mint.

Bring a large pot of salted water to a boil, add the shrimp, and cook until they are pink, about 2 minutes. Remove from heat, drain, and rinse in cold water. Remove the shells.

Toss the shrimp with the lime juice mixture and allow to marinate 15–20 minutes in the refrigerator.

Serves 4

$3/4$ cup fresh lime juice

1 teaspoon red pepper flakes

3 cloves garlic, finely chopped

$2/3$ cup fish sauce (see Sources, page 77)

2 tablespoons finely chopped cilantro leaves

2 tablespoons finely chopped mint leaves

1 pound small shrimp

Herbed Deviled Eggs

XXXXXX

Makes 2 dozen

12 eggs

½ cup Cilantro Aioli (see page 29)

Salt

24 small sprigs of cilantro

Deviled eggs are a great last-minute dish. This recipe makes a lot, but on the slim chance you have leftovers, just mash them up for egg salad sandwiches, adding more aioli if needed.

Bring a large pot of water to a boil. Gently add the eggs and cook 12 minutes.

Drain and transfer the eggs to a large bowl of ice water.

When the eggs are cool enough to handle, peel and halve them. Transfer the yolks to a bowl and mash them with the Cilantro Aioli, adding salt to taste.

Using a spoon, melon baller, or pastry bag, fill the egg-white halves with the yolk mixture. Garnish each with a sprig of cilantro before serving.

Seven-Layer Dip

xxxxxx

A classic party dish, this dip may cause you to veer dangerously off the course of your diet. If you have a trifle bowl or other tall-sided clear glass bowl, you can use it to great effect here. Feel free to substitute pepper Jack cheese for the Cheddar, tomatillos for the tomatoes, or pickled jalapeños for the black olives.

Spread the refried beans in a thick layer on the bottom of a clear glass dish. Follow with layers of sour cream, guacamole, cheese, tomatoes, green onions, and black olives. Finish with a final layer of sour cream and garnish with cilantro sprigs.

Serves 12

2 cups refried pinto or black beans

1 cup sour cream

1 cup Chunky Guacamole (see page 22)

1 cup shredded Cheddar cheese

$1/2$ cup diced tomatoes

$1/2$ cup sliced green onions

$1/2$ cup sliced black olives

$1/4$ cup cilantro sprigs, for garnish

Crab Cakes with Cilantro Aioli

xxxxxx

These cakes get much of their flavor from the inclusion of Cilantro Aioli. You can serve them with Chunky Guacamole, Charred Tomatillo Salsa, or more of the aioli.

Carefully inspect the crabmeat and remove any pieces of cartilage or shell.

In a bowl, beat together the aioli, egg, and salt. Add the crab, bell pepper, and green onion, and toss well. Add just enough bread crumbs to allow you to form the mixture into 4 large patties.

Heat the peanut oil in a heavy skillet and fry the patties until cooked through and golden brown on both sides.

Serves 4

1 pound lump crabmeat

$1/4$ cup Cilantro Aioli (recipe follows)

1 egg

$1/2$ teaspoon salt

$1/4$ cup finely chopped red bell pepper

$1/4$ cup finely chopped green onion

Approximately $1/2$ cup fresh bread crumbs

$1/4$ cup peanut oil

CILANTRO AIOLI

In a bowl, combine the mayonnaise, garlic, cilantro, lime juice, and jalapeño. Add salt to taste.

Makes about 1⅓ cups

1 cup mayonnaise

1 clove garlic, finely chopped

2 tablespoons finely chopped cilantro leaves

$1/4$ cup lime juice

1 jalapeño (optional)

Salt

Herb-filled Fresh Spring Rolls

xxxxxx

Makes 8 rolls

½ **pound shrimp**

4 **ounces rice vermicelli
(see Sources, page 77)**

8 **large rice paper wrappers
(see Sources, page 77)**

½ **cup fresh basil leaves**

½ **cup fresh mint leaves**

½ **cup fresh cilantro leaves**

½ **cup hoisin sauce (see
Sources, page 77)**

2 **teaspoons warm water**

1 **tablespoon finely
chopped roasted peanuts**

These Vietnamese snacks are known by many names, but the standard way to distinguish them from deep-fried spring rolls is to simply call them fresh spring rolls.

Bring a pot of salted water to a boil, add the shrimp, and cook until they are completely pink and firm. Remove from heat, drain, and rinse them in cold water. Remove the shells.

Bring another pot of water to a boil and add the rice vermicelli. Cook until al dente, 3–5 minutes. Drain and set aside to cool.

Fill a large, shallow bowl with warm water. Submerge a rice paper wrapper in the water for a few seconds until it softens and becomes pliable. Spread the wrapper flat on a large plate. In the middle of the wrapper, arrange some of the noodles, basil, mint, cilantro, and shrimp. Fold it up like a burrito, bringing the sides toward the middle, then rolling to seal.

In a small bowl, stir together hoisin sauce, warm water, and roasted peanuts. Serve the spring rolls with this dipping sauce.

Salads

xxxxx

Orange Jicama Salad

xxxxxx

Serves 4–6

1 medium-size jicama

4 navel oranges

Cilantro sprigs

Salt and freshly
ground black pepper

1 teaspoon chile
powder (optional)

Juice of 1 lime

Extra-virgin olive oil

This salad is a play on insalata Caprese, *the Italian salad with tomatoes, mozzarella, and basil. This version is just as cool and refreshing. It also travels well, so try it for a summer potluck.*

Use a vegetable peeler to remove the thick peel from the jicama. Slice into ¼-inch-thick discs, then quarter each disc.

Use a knife to slice off all of the orange peels and white pith. Slice the oranges into ¼-inch-thick discs.

On a platter, arrange alternating jicama slices, cilantro sprigs, and orange discs. Sprinkle with salt, pepper, chile powder, lime juice, and olive oil. Let rest 20 minutes before serving.

Wild Rice Salad with Golden Raisins, Pistachios, and Pomegranate Vinaigrette
XXXXXX

This dish is an excellent accompaniment to grilled meats but is substantial enough to make a meal by itself. Be warned that the pistachios will lose their crunchy texture if left in the salad too long, so add them just before serving.

In a large bowl, combine the wild and white rice, green onions, raisins, and cilantro.

In another bowl, combine the garlic, lemon juice, and pomegranate molasses. Whisking constantly, add the olive oil in a thin stream, until the mixture is thick and creamy. Add to rice mixture and toss to coat. Season with salt and pepper to taste, adding the pistachios last.

Serves 8–10

2 cups cooked wild rice, cooled

4 cups cooked white rice, cooled

1 cup thinly sliced green onions

1 cup golden raisins

1/2 cup finely chopped cilantro

1 clove garlic, finely chopped

Juice of 1 lemon

1 tablespoon pomegranate molasses (see Sources, page 77)

1/2 cup extra-virgin olive oil

Salt and freshly ground black pepper

1 cup roasted and shelled pistachio nuts

Mediterranean Lamb Salad
with Cilantro Balsamic Vinaigrette

xxxxxx

Serves 4

Use leftovers from a lamb roast to make this cool but satisfying salad.

1 head romaine lettuce (about 1 pound), washed, dried, and chopped

1 medium cucumber, peeled, seeded, and sliced

1 small red onion, halved and sliced into half-moons

1 pint cherry tomatoes, halved

1/2 cup sliced black olives

1/2 cup crumbled feta cheese

Cilantro Balsamic Vinaigrette (recipe follows)

Salt and freshly ground black pepper

1 pound cooked lamb, sliced thin

In a large bowl, toss together the lettuce, cucumber, onion, tomatoes, olives, and feta. Add the vinaigrette and toss again. Season with salt and pepper to taste. Top with strips of lamb and serve.

CILANTRO BALSAMIC VINAIGRETTE

1 clove garlic, finely chopped

3 tablespoons balsamic vinegar

2 tablespoons finely chopped mint

2 tablespoons finely chopped cilantro

2/3 cup extra-virgin olive oil

In a bowl, combine the garlic, vinegar, mint, and cilantro. Whisking constantly, add the olive oil in a thin stream until the mixture is thick and creamy.

Curried Chicken Salad with Mango and Cashews

xxxxxx

This quick and easy chicken salad can be served as a sandwich or the low-carbohydrate way—on a bed of greens. You can use a store-bought rotisserie chicken for this recipe, but choose one without any added flavorings.

In a large bowl, combine the mayonnaise and curry powder. Add the chicken, mango, shallot, cilantro, and cashews; toss to combine. Depending on the chicken and the curry powder, you may not need to add any salt.

Serves 4–8

$1/3$ cup mayonnaise

1 teaspoon Madras curry powder

4 cups chopped cooked chicken

1 large mango, peeled, seeded, and diced

1 large shallot, chopped

$1/3$ cup chopped cilantro leaves

$1/3$ cup coarsely chopped roasted cashews

Salt, if needed

Southwestern Coleslaw

xxxxxx

People who dislike mayonnaise will appreciate this tangy/sweet slaw. As with any slaw, it will be too dry as soon as it's finished and too wet if you leave it in the refrigerator overnight. Let it rest an hour or so, then serve it on fish tacos or as a side dish with barbecued meat.

In a bowl, combine the lime juice, honey, cumin, and chile. Stir until the honey is completely dissolved.

In a large bowl, toss the shredded green and red cabbage with the cilantro and prepared dressing. Season to taste with salt and pepper. Cover and refrigerate at least 1 hour. Taste and adjust seasonings, if necessary.

Serves 8–12

$1/4$ cup lime juice

1 tablespoon honey

$1/2$ teaspoon ground cumin

1 jalapeño chile (optional)

1 pound green cabbage, finely shredded (about 3 cups)

1 pound red cabbage, finely shredded (about 3 cups)

$1/2$ cup finely chopped cilantro leaves

Salt and freshly ground black pepper

Shredded Beet Salad with Lemony Cilantro Vinaigrette

xxxxxx

Serves 4

4 medium beets

¼ cup Lemony Cilantro Vinaigrette (recipe follows)

Salt and freshly ground black pepper

I once interviewed Mark Bittman, author of How to Cook Everything, *for a newspaper story. During the interview, I asked him about the easiest way to cook beets, and he responded that the easiest way to serve beets was not to cook them at all, but to finely shred the tough vegetables and toss them with a vinaigrette. It was a revelation. I love beets, but now I rarely cook them, getting my fix from quick salads like this. Feel free to add shredded carrots or cucumber to the beets. For a more substantial salad, serve on a bed of lettuce dressed in the same vinaigrette.*

Peel the beets and shred them, using a hand-held grater or the shredding disc on your food processor.

Toss with vinaigrette, season with salt and pepper, and serve chilled.

Makes about ½ cup

1 teaspoon finely grated lemon zest

2 tablespoons lemon juice

2 tablespoons finely chopped cilantro

1 finely chopped shallot

6 tablespoons extra-virgin olive oil

LEMONY CILANTRO VINAIGRETTE

Put the lemon zest, lemon juice, cilantro, and shallot into a bowl. Whisking constantly, add the olive oil in a thin stream.

Iceberg Wedges with Creamy Cilantro Dressing

xxxxxx

Cool, crunchy iceberg lettuce is extraordinarily refreshing on a hot summer day, especially with this rich, herbed dressing. Use extra dressing as a dip for vegetables and potato chips.

Wash the lettuce well and cut the head in half. Carefully remove the core and cut each piece in half again, making 4 wedges. Slice a silver-dollar-size piece from the curved surface of each lettuce wedge and it won't wobble on the plate.

Sprinkle each lettuce wedge with salt and pepper, then drizzle the dressing over the wedges and garnish with cilantro sprigs.

Serves 4

1 large head iceberg lettuce

Salt and pepper

$\frac{1}{2}$ cup Creamy Cilantro Dressing (recipe follows)

4 sprigs cilantro

CREAMY CILANTRO DRESSING

In a bowl, whisk together all ingredients. Cover and store in the refrigerator until ready to use.

Makes 1½ cups

$3/4$ cup mayonnaise

$3/4$ cup buttermilk

2 tablespoons finely chopped cilantro leaves

1 tablespoon fresh lime juice

1 clove garlic, finely chopped

Salt and pepper

Tabbouleh with Cilantro and Feta

xxxxxx

Serves 6

This Middle Eastern salad is usually made with parsley, but I think it's even better with cilantro and mint.

3 cups water

2 cups bulgur

Bring the water to a boil.

¹/₂ cup finely chopped cilantro leaves

¹/₂ cup finely chopped mint leaves

Put the bulgur into a large heat-safe bowl. Pour the boiling water over the bulgur and let it stand for 45 minutes.

¹/₃ cup lemon juice

³/₄ cup olive oil

Toss the bulgur with the cilantro, mint, lemon juice, olive oil, tomatoes, onion, and feta. Season with salt and pepper to taste. Serve at room temperature or chilled.

2 large ripe tomatoes, cored and diced

¹/₂ cup diced onion

1 cup crumbled feta cheese

Salt and freshly ground black pepper

Tomato Soup with Fresh Corn Salsa and Chipotle Cream

xxxxxx

Serves 6

3 tablespoons
extra-virgin olive oil

2 pounds ripe
tomatoes, cored

6 sprigs cilantro

2 cloves garlic,
finely chopped

Salt and freshly
ground pepper

3 cups Fresh Corn Salsa
(see page 16)

1 cup Chipotle Cream
(recipe follows)

Make this simple soup in the summer, when local tomatoes are plentiful and inexpensive. By not boiling the tomatoes, you can preserve their fresh flavor. One big batch will last a week in the refrigerator and can be served with a number of different garnishes.

In a stainless steel or enameled cast-iron stockpot, combine the olive oil, tomatoes, cilantro, and garlic. Do not bring to a boil, but cook over medium-low heat until the tomatoes soften, about 20 minutes.

Over a large bowl, press the tomatoes through a mesh strainer to remove the seeds and skins. Season with salt and pepper to taste.

Serve this soup chilled or at room temperature, garnished with Fresh Corn Salsa and a dollop of Chipotle Cream.

CHIPOTLE CREAM

Makes 1 cup

1 cup sour cream (or
substitute nonfat
plain yogurt)

1 chile from a can of
chipotles in adobo sauce,
chopped (see Sources,
page 77)

In a bowl, combine the sour cream and chopped chipotle. Add liquid from the can until the desired heat level is reached.

Chilled Avocado Soup

xxxxxx

Use a high-quality, low-sodium chicken broth for this soup. I prefer Swanson Natural Goodness, but whichever you choose, use it every time you make this soup or the flavor will be noticeably different. If you wish, this soup can be garnished with any fresh salsa.

In a blender, puree the avocados, chicken broth, and cilantro. Add lime juice and salt to taste.

Serves 4 as a first course

2 large ripe avocados, peeled, pitted, and chopped

2 cups chicken broth

2 tablespoons finely chopped cilantro leaves

Juice of 1 lime, or more, to taste

Salt

Gazpacho

xxxxxx

Don't be tempted to make this soup when you can't find perfectly ripe tomatoes. It's not worth even the minimal effort of making it.

In a blender or food processor, process the tomatoes, cucumbers, onion, and bell peppers until blended but still slightly chunky. Do not puree.

Pour the mixture into a large glass pitcher. Stir in the lime juice, garlic, jalapeños (if using), and cilantro. Season with salt and pepper to taste.

Chill for at least 1 hour to allow the flavors to blend. Serve with warm, crusty bread.

Serves 8

2½ pounds perfectly ripe tomatoes

2 medium cucumbers, peeled and seeded

1 large red onion, coarsely chopped

2 red, yellow, or orange bell peppers, seeded and coarsely chopped

Juice of 2 limes or lemons

3 cloves garlic, finely chopped

2 jalapeños, seeded and finely chopped (optional)

¼ cup finely chopped cilantro leaves

Salt and freshly ground black pepper

8 pieces warm, crusty bread

Red Chile Pork Posole

xxxxxx

Serves 8–10

2 cups dried hominy (see
Sources, page 77)

1 large onion, diced

1 tablespoon finely
chopped garlic

2 tablespoons olive
oil or lard

1 pound pork
stew-meat cubes

2 dried New Mexico
chile pods, stemmed,
seeded, and chopped
(see Sources, page 77)

$\frac{1}{4}$ teaspoon ground cloves

1 teaspoon salt

$\frac{1}{2}$ cup finely chopped
cilantro, for garnish

1 cup diced onion,
for garnish

Here is some real Southwestern comfort food. Make it when you'll be home all day and are expecting a crowd for dinner. You can substitute canned hominy for dried posole (it's the same thing and is often sold in the Southwest as "nixtamal"), but canned hominy can be a bit soggy. Serve with warm flour tortillas on the side.

Put the hominy in a large bowl and cover with plenty of lightly salted water. Allow to soak overnight.

In a large stockpot, sauté the onions and garlic in oil or lard. Add the pork and cook until the cubes are browned on all sides. Remove the meat from the pot and set aside.

Now put into the same pot the chiles, cloves, salt, drained hominy, and enough water to cover. Bring to a boil, then reduce heat to low and simmer at least 3 hours, or until the hominy kernels are puffy and tender. Add more water if necessary.

Add the cooked pork and cook 30 minutes longer.

Serve hot and garnish with cilantro and onion.

Tortilla Soup

xxxxxx

I like to use chicken thighs for this recipe, because they have more flavor than chicken breasts.

In a large stockpot, heat the 2 tablespoons of corn oil. Sprinkle salt and pepper over the chicken and place the chicken in the pot. Sauté, meaty side down, about 2 minutes. Turn the chicken and add the onion, tomato, and garlic. Continue cooking about 2 more minutes.

Add the chicken broth. Bring the soup to a boil, then reduce the heat and simmer until the chicken is cooked through, about 15 minutes.

Meanwhile, in a heavy skillet, fry the tortilla strips in the cup of corn oil until golden and crispy. Allow the tortilla strips to drain on a paper-towel–lined plate.

Remove the chicken thighs from the soup and, with two forks, separate the meat from the bones.

Divide the chicken evenly among 6 bowls. Pour the broth over the chicken. Garnish with cilantro, lime juice, and the prepared tortilla strips.

Serves 6

2 tablespoons corn oil

Salt and freshly ground black pepper

3 chicken thighs (bone in but skin removed)

½ large onion, chopped

1 tomato, chopped and seeded

2 cloves garlic, finely chopped

6 cups high-quality, low-sodium chicken broth

3 corn tortillas, sliced into ribbons

1 cup corn oil

2 tablespoons finely chopped fresh cilantro

2 tablespoons lime juice

Carrot Soup with Coriander Seed and Cilantro

XXXXXX

Serves 6

4 tablespoons (½ stick)
unsalted butter

1 large onion,
peeled and diced

3 cloves garlic,
finely chopped

2 pounds carrots, peeled
and roughly chopped

2 teaspoons
ground coriander

6 cups high-quality,
low-sodium chicken
or vegetable broth

½ cup finely
chopped cilantro

Salt and freshly
ground black pepper

Cilantro sprigs, for garnish

This soup can be served year-round, as it is equally tasty hot or cold. The easiest way to puree soups like this is to use a hand-held blender to puree the soup right in the cooking pot. If you don't have one, you can process the soup in batches in a blender. Consider garnishing it with a dollop of Chipotle Cream (see page 44).

In a large stockpot, melt the butter. Add the onion and sauté until softened. Add the garlic and sauté 1 minute longer. Add the carrots and cook, stirring, until the carrots are heated through.

Add the coriander and broth and bring the mixture to a boil, then reduce the heat and simmer about 30 minutes, or until the carrots are tender. Remove from heat.

Add the chopped cilantro and use a hand-held blender to puree the soup. Season with salt and pepper to taste, pour into bowls, and garnish with cilantro sprigs.

Main Dishes

xxxxxx

Buffalo Burgers with Pepita Pesto

xxxxxx

Makes 4 burgers

1 pound ground buffalo meat

¼ cup Pepita Pesto (recipe follows)

4 hearty rolls, split

3 tablespoons olive oil

Lettuce, tomato, avocado, and onion for garnish

Buffalo meat is very lean, and it benefits from the rich flavor of this pumpkin seed (pepita) pesto. You can use any leftover pesto on black beans or nachos, or tossed with pasta.

Preheat a charcoal or gas grill.

In a large bowl, combine the meat and pesto. Form the mixture into 4 patties. Grill over medium heat until the burgers reach the desired level of doneness.

Brush the rolls with the olive oil and toast them on the grill until golden.

Serve the burgers garnished with lettuce, tomato, avocado, and onion.

PEPITA PESTO

Makes about 2 cups

½ cup pumpkin seeds (without shells)

2 cups coarsely chopped cilantro leaves

3 cloves garlic, finely chopped

¼ cup grated Parmesan cheese

¼ cup extra-virgin olive oil

Salt and freshly ground pepper

In a heavy skillet over medium-high heat, toast the pumpkin seeds until most of them are puffed. Remove them from the heat and allow them to cool.

In a blender or food processor, process the cilantro, garlic, toasted pumpkin seeds, and Parmesan. Add the olive oil in a thin stream. Season to taste with salt and pepper.

Use immediately or store in the refrigerator for up to a week.

Crying Tiger (Steak with Chile-Cilantro Sauce)

xxxxxx

This grilled beef dish is a common sight on Thai restaurant menus. It is normally made with so much chile that it would make even a tiger cry. Feel free to use as much—or as little— cayenne as you like. The meat is usually sliced into bite-size pieces and served over lettuce, but you can also serve the steaks whole.

In a large bowl, marinate the steaks in the soy sauce for at least 30 minutes.

Mix together the lime juice, fish sauce, brown sugar, cayenne, shallots, and cilantro, and set aside.

Drain the steaks and pat them dry. Grill over medium heat until they reach the desired level of doneness. Allow the steaks to rest 10 minutes before serving.

Pour a little of the sauce over the meat, then offer the rest on the side.

Serves 4

4 New York strip steaks, trimmed of excess fat

$^1/_2$ **cup soy sauce**

$^1/_2$ **cup lime juice**

$^1/_2$ **cup fish sauce**

1 tablespoon brown sugar

$^1/_2$ **teaspoon cayenne pepper**

3 shallots, finely chopped

$^1/_4$ **cup finely chopped cilantro leaves**

Mexican
Style Flank
Steak
$9.99 LB

Mexican Flank Steak

xxxxxx

This recipe was graciously provided by AJ's Fine Foods in Tucson, Arizona.

Preheat the oven to 350 degrees F. Lightly coat the inside of each steak with roasted red bell pepper pesto, then lay the steaks edge to edge, slightly overlapping. Place a row of 1-inch-thick slices of pepper Jack cheese down the center of the steaks, followed by the julienned yellow, red, and orange bell peppers, the julienned poblano pepper, and the cilantro. Roll this up so the cheese slices are in the middle, and tie it up with string.

Before placing the meat in the roasting pan, pour a little red wine into the bottom of the pan and insert a meat thermometer horizontally into the rolled flank so that it touches only the meat and not any of the other ingredients rolled inside. Roast either covered or uncovered for about 12–15 minutes per pound, until the internal temperature reaches 110 degrees F.

Cut into ½- to ¾-inch slices for a nice serving size. Pour the pan drippings, which will include some of the cheese, over the slices.

Serves 5–6

2 trimmed flank steaks, tenderized (about 2½–3½ pounds)

8 ounces roasted red bell pepper pesto

8 ounces pepper Jack cheese

½ yellow bell pepper, julienned

½ red bell pepper, julienned

½ orange bell pepper, julienned

½ poblano pepper, julienned (seeds removed)

2 bunches fresh cilantro sprigs (stems removed, chopped)

Red wine

BLTs with Chipotle Mayo

xxxxxx

Makes 2

1/4 cup mayonnaise

1/2 chipotle chile in adobo sauce, finely chopped (see Sources, page 77)

4 slices sandwich bread, toasted

Iceberg lettuce

6 pieces cooked bacon

1 large tomato

Cilantro sprigs

In this sandwich, the smoky flavors of bacon and chipotle are offset by cold tomatoes, crisp lettuce, and cilantro sprigs.

In a small bowl, stir together the mayonnaise and chipotle, adjusting the heat level by adding more juice from the can of chiles or more mayonnaise.

Slather the toasted bread with chipotle mayo, then add lettuce, bacon, tomato slices, and cilantro sprigs.

Barbecued Chicken and Manchego Pizza

xxxxxx

Serves 4

1 ready-to-bake pizza crust

1/2 cup of your favorite barbecue sauce

1/2 cup cilantro leaves

2 1/2 cups cooked, shredded chicken

1 1/2 cups shredded manchego cheese

Here is one of my absolute favorite kinds of pizza—sweet, tangy, and decidedly unconventional. You can make your own pizza dough or buy one of those ready-to-bake crusts, such as Boboli.

Preheat the oven to 475 degrees F.

Use a spatula to spread the barbecue sauce over the surface of the dough, leaving a 1-inch border of un-sauced dough around the edges. Sprinkle the dough with the cilantro leaves, then with the shredded chicken and cheese.

Bake about 15 minutes, or until the crust is golden-brown. Remove from the oven and allow to cool briefly before transferring to a cutting board. Slice and serve with a green salad.

Linguine with Cilantro Pesto

xxxxxx

You can add seafood, chicken, tofu, or pretty much anything to this pasta, but why bother? This simple dish is anything but plain.

Bring a large pot of salted water to a boil. Add the linguine and cook according to the package instructions.

Drain the pasta, leaving a little water in the bottom of the pot. Add the pesto to the pot and toss with the pasta to combine. Season with salt and pepper and serve.

Serves 6–8

1 pound linguine

3/4–1 cup Cilantro Pesto (recipe follows)

Salt and pepper

CILANTRO PESTO

In a blender or food processor, puree all the ingredients together. Store in the refrigerator, wrapped tightly, for up to a week. You can also double this batch, spoon the extra pesto into ice cube trays, freeze, and store for later.

Makes about 1 cup

2 cups firmly packed cilantro leaves

1/2 cup extra-virgin olive oil

3 cloves garlic, finely chopped

1/3 cup toasted piñon nuts

Zest and juice of 1 lime

Grilled Pork Tenderloin
with Dried Apricot Chutney

xxxxxx

Serves 4

Serve the tenderloin over fluffy basmati rice. Make sandwiches with leftover pork, chutney, and wedges of Brie cheese.

2 tablespoons Dijon mustard

1 tablespoon ground cumin

1 tablespoon ground coriander

1 teaspoon salt

1 teaspoon freshly ground black pepper

1 pork tenderloin (1 1/2 pounds)

Dried Apricot Chutney (recipe follows)

Preheat a gas or charcoal grill.

In a bowl, combine the mustard, cumin, coriander, salt, and pepper. Rub the mustard mixture all over the pork.

Over medium heat, grill the pork, turning frequently, until it is cooked but still a little pink in the middle. Remove from the heat and allow to rest 10 minutes.

Slice the pork into ½-inch-thick rounds and spoon warm apricot chutney over it.

DRIED APRICOT CHUTNEY

Makes about 2 cups

8 ounces dried apricots

1 onion, roughly chopped

1 cup cilantro leaves

1/4 teaspoon ground cloves

4 tablespoons finely chopped gingerroot

1/3 cup apple cider vinegar

1/3 cup honey

Salt

In the workbowl of a food processor, combine the apricots, onion, cilantro, cloves, and gingerroot. Pulse until the mixture is combined but still very chunky—don't work it into a paste.

Transfer the apricot mixture to a medium saucepan. Add the vinegar and honey, and bring the mixture to a boil. Reduce to a simmer and cook until the onions and apricots are softened. Add water to thin if the mixture is too thick. Add salt to taste.

Roasted Chicken with Cilantro-Lime Rub

xxxxxx

With the ubiquity of rotisserie chickens in supermarkets, it is tempting to give up roasting your own. Resist the urge. Especially if you can use a locally raised chicken, the results blow away supermarket birds.

Preheat the oven to 425 degrees F.

Rinse the chicken with cold water, then pat it dry, and remove any excess fat. Sprinkle salt and pepper on the inside and outside of the bird.

In a bowl, combine the cilantro, garlic, red pepper flakes, lime juice, and 2 tablespoons of the olive oil.

Use your hand to gently separate the chicken skin from the breast and thighs. Spread the cilantro paste between the skin and the meat. Slather the remaining tablespoon of olive oil over the outside of the chicken.

Place chicken on a rack in a roasting pan. Roast about 1 hour, or until the skin is golden brown and the temperature of the thickest part of the thigh is 165 degrees F.

Remove chicken from oven, tent loosely with foil and allow to rest about 15 minutes.

Carve and serve with pan juices.

Serves 2–4

1 roasting chicken

Salt and freshly ground black pepper

$1/3$ cup chopped cilantro

3 cloves garlic, finely chopped

$1/2$ teaspoon red pepper flakes

Juice of $1/2$ lime

3 tablespoons olive oil

Chile-braised Lamb Shanks
with Cilantro Gremolata

xxxxxx

Serves 4

1 pound dried red chiles
(New Mexico, pasilla, or
guajillo; see Sources,
page 77)

4 cloves garlic,
finely chopped

2 teaspoons ground cumin

Juice of 1 lemon

$1/2$ teaspoon salt

4 lamb shanks

2 cups dark beer
(such as Negro Modelo)

Cilantro Gremolata
(recipe follows)

This is based on a recipe developed by the American Lamb Board. I added the gremolata (a pungent cilantro and lemon garnish). It is normally made with parsley and used with osso buco, *the Italian dish of braised veal shanks. Because lamb shanks are so much smaller than veal shanks, use one whole shank per person. Serve with beautiful Creamed Corn Tamales (see page 67) or mashed potatoes.*

Preheat the oven to 350 degrees F.

Arrange the chiles on a baking sheet and toast 2–5 minutes, until they smell toasted but before they burn. Remove them from the oven and set aside.

When the chiles are cool enough to handle, remove the stems and seeds. Tear the chiles into pieces and put them into a large saucepan. Add enough water to cover, bring to a boil, then turn off the heat and allow the chiles to soak until completely softened.

Drain off and reserve most of the water. Transfer the chiles to a blender and process, adding just enough water to make a thick, smooth paste. Strain the mixture through a fine sieve. Add the garlic, cumin, lemon juice, and salt.

Trim any excess fat from the lamb shanks. Slather the meat with the chile paste and let it marinate in the refrigerator overnight.

Preheat the oven to 325 degrees F.

Place the meat in a deep roasting pan. Add the beer and enough water to come halfway up the sides of the shanks. Cover pan with foil and cook until the meat is very tender.

Remove the shanks from the pan. Skim the fat from the pan drippings and whisk in enough water to make a rich sauce.

Serve the lamb with plenty of sauce, garnished with Cilantro Gremolata (recipe follows).

CILANTRO GREMOLATA

Combine all ingredients in a small bowl.

3 tablespoons finely chopped cilantro leaves

3 cloves garlic, finely chopped

Finely grated zest of 1 large lemon

Flank Steak with Creamy Rajas

xxxxxx

Serves 4

1 pound fresh
poblano chiles

1 large onion, peeled

1 tablespoon butter

1/2 cup heavy cream

1 flank steak (1 1/2 pounds),
trimmed of excess fat

1/2 teaspoon ground cumin

1/2 teaspoon
ground coriander

Salt and freshly
ground black pepper

8 flour tortillas

The sliced peppers that accompany this steak are called rajas *in Spanish. You can use poblanos or New Mexico green chiles for this recipe. Both work well.*

Over a gas flame, under a broiler, or on a grill, roast the chiles until they are dark and blistered. Place them in a bowl and cover with plastic wrap until they are cool enough to handle. Remove the stems, seeds, and charred skin, and slice the chiles into 1/2-inch-wide strips. Set them aside.

Slice the onion in half from the stem to the root end. Slice into 1/2-inch-wide strips.

In a heavy skillet, melt the butter and sauté the onions until they are softened and starting to brown. Add the chiles. Add the cream and simmer for 5 minutes, or until the mixture thickens.

Sprinkle the flank steak with cumin, coriander, salt, and pepper. Grill or broil for 5–8 minutes on each side, or until it reaches the desired level of doneness. Remove from the heat and allow to rest 10 minutes.

Holding your knife at a 45-degree angle, slice the steak into thin strips. Serve with warm tortillas and creamy rajas.

Salmon in a Packet with Moroccan Charmoula

xxxxxx

Wild-caught Alaskan salmon is high in healthy Omega-3 fatty acids, low in mercury, and just plain delicious, especially when topped with charmoula, an exotic North African sauce. Serve with hot couscous and grilled vegetables.

In a bowl or other container large enough to hold the salmon, mix together the cumin, coriander, paprika, chile powder, salt, cilantro, garlic, lemon juice, lime juice, and olive oil. Add the salmon to the bowl, slather with charmoula, and allow it to marinate for 20 minutes in the refrigerator.

Preheat the oven to 350 degrees F.

On a flat work surface, lay out 2 sheets of heavy-duty aluminum foil, 1½ feet long, to make a double-thick packet. Place the salmon in the middle of the foil and top with more of the charmoula. Fold the foil over the fish and crimp the edges to form a tight seal.

Bake the salmon for 15–20 minutes, or until the fish at the thickest part is opaque almost all the way through. Remove from the oven, open the packet, and cut into 6–8 pieces.

Serves 6–8

1 tablespoon ground cumin

1½ teaspoons ground coriander

1 tablespoon paprika

1 tablespoon red chile powder

1 teaspoon salt

½ cup chopped cilantro leaves

4 cloves garlic, finely chopped

¼ cup lemon juice

¼ cup lime juice

⅓ cup extra-virgin olive oil

1 side of salmon (3–4 pounds)

Grilled Ginger Chicken with Star Fruit

xxxxxx

Star fruit, also known as carambola, is a yellowish-green fruit roughly the size of a fat dill pickle. Slices of the fruit are star-shaped and have a tart, citrusy flavor. If you can't find them, make the chicken anyway; it's delicious even without the star fruit. Serve with basmati rice.

Place each chicken breast, one at a time, between two sheets of plastic wrap and pound with a mallet to an even ½-inch thickness. This will ensure that the pieces cook evenly on the grill.

In a large bowl, combine the gingerroot, garlic, jalapeño, olive oil, and cilantro. Add the chicken and star fruit slices. Marinate at least 1 hour or overnight.

Preheat a charcoal or gas grill. Sprinkle the chicken with salt and pepper. Over medium heat, grill the chicken breasts for 5 minutes on each side. Remove the chicken to a platter and grill the star fruit slices until brown and softened.

Serves 6

2 pounds boneless, skinless chicken breasts

1 tablespoon finely chopped fresh gingerroot

3 cloves garlic, finely chopped

1 jalapeño chile, stemmed, seeded, and finely chopped

2 tablespoons olive oil

½ cup finely chopped cilantro leaves

1 star fruit, sliced ¼-inch-thick

Salt and freshly ground black pepper

Migas

xxxxxx

Serves 4–6

3 tablespoons butter

4 small corn tortillas, torn
into bite-size pieces

$1/2$ cup diced onion

$1/2$ cup diced red bell pepper

$1/2$ cup roasted, peeled,
and diced green chiles (see
page 13 for roasting tips)

12 eggs, lightly beaten

$1/4$ cup finely
chopped cilantro

$1/2$ pound chorizo,
cooked and drained

1 cup Pico de Gallo
(see page 14)

This Southwestern breakfast dish makes good use of leftover tortillas. If you don't have any corn tortillas, you can also use pieces of stale tortilla chips.

In a heavy skillet, melt the butter. Fry the tortilla pieces until softened. Add the onion, bell pepper, and green chiles, and sauté until the onion is softened.

Add the eggs and cilantro, and cook, stirring well, until the eggs are mostly done. Add the chorizo and cook 2 minutes longer. Remove from heat. Serve garnished with Pico de Gallo.

Calabacitas

xxxxxx

Serves 4–6

4 tablespoons
(½ stick) butter

½ cup chopped onion

2 small zucchini
(about ½ pound), diced

2 small yellow
summer squash (about ½
pound), diced

Approximately 1½ cups corn
kernels (about 2 large ears)

2 roasted and peeled New
Mexico or Anaheim green
chiles, chopped

Salt

1 cup shredded Monterey
Jack or Cheddar cheese

½ cup chopped
cilantro leaves

Make this dish in the late summer when corn, squash, and chiles are all found at farmers markets and roadside stands. You can also wrap these calabacitas up into vegetarian burritos.

In a large skillet over medium heat, melt the butter. Add the onion, zucchini, and summer squash, and cook for 5 minutes. Add the corn and green chiles, and continue cooking until the zucchini and summer squash are tender. Add salt to taste.

Remove from heat, toss with cheese and cilantro, and serve hot.

Creamed Corn Tamales

xxxxxx

These tamales aren't made with the traditional masa harina, *but with coarse cornmeal, so they have a lighter, less dense consistency. Cilantro sprigs are pressed into the dough before cooking and are exposed when the tamales are opened. These are fabulous served with Mango Habanero Salsa (see page 14). You can use husks from fresh corn cobs or buy dried husks for these, but either way, buy many more husks than you think you'll need; some will be too small, some will rip, and others will be too thin. You will also need a steamer to cook these tamales. If you don't have one, you can fill the bottom of your largest pot with wadded-up balls of aluminum foil. Pour water halfway up the foil balls and rest the tamales on top of them.*

Makes 8

About 30 corn husks

3 cups high-quality, low-sodium chicken or vegetable stock

1 cup coarse cornmeal

1 cup creamed corn

2 New Mexico green chiles, roasted, peeled, seeded, and chopped

8–12 perfect (3-inch-long) cilantro sprigs

If you're using dried corn husks, put them in a tall pitcher filled with warm water, and allow them to soften while you prepare the cornmeal.

In a large stockpot, bring the stock to a boil. Sprinkle in the cornmeal while whisking constantly. Reduce heat to low and cook, stirring constantly with a whisk, then a spoon, for about 10 minutes, or until the mixture thickens and all of the water is absorbed.

Remove from the heat, stir in the creamed corn and green chiles, and allow the mixture to rest about 10 minutes.

Remove 1 husk from the soaking water and shake off any excess water. Lay the husk flat on a work surface. Scoop about ½ cup of the corn mixture from the pot and scrape it out on to the middle of the husk, in roughly the shape of a rectangle, then press a cilantro sprig into the surface. Fold the bottom of the husk up over the filling, then fold the top of the husk down. Rotate the tamale and fold the sides in over the center. Now tear a long strip from one of the softened husks and use it to tie a belt around the middle of the folded tamale. Repeat until all of the corn mixture is used.

Fill the bottom of your steamer with water and bring to a boil. Put the tamales in the steamer and cook 15 minutes, or until they are firm.

Serve hot and still wrapped, with any fresh-fruit salsa or chile sauce on the side.

Grilled Corn with Lime Cilantro Butter

xxxxxx

Grilled corn is one of the finest summer pleasures. I think the easiest way to cook it is also one of the tastiest; put it right on the grill, still in the husk. Extra lime cilantro butter can be dotted on other cooked vegetables, steaks, even popcorn. The Cilantro Lime Butter recipe makes twice as much as you'll need for 6 ears of corn, but if wrapped tightly, it will keep for several weeks in the freezer.

Serves 6

6 ears fresh corn, husks on

6 tablespoons Lime Cilantro Butter (recipe follows)

Preheat a gas or charcoal grill.

Peel back the first few layers of corn husk, but leave most inner layers intact. Put the cobs on the grill and cook, turning often, until the husks are completely charred, about 10 minutes.

Remove from grill and pull the husks off, brushing away any corn silk or charred husk. Serve hot, with plenty of Lime Cilantro Butter.

LIME CILANTRO BUTTER

In a bowl, combine the butter, cilantro, shallot, and chile powder.

Makes ½ cup

Scrape the butter out onto a large piece of wax paper. Use the wax paper to roll the butter up into a log about 1½ inches in diameter. Chill until firm.

1 stick (8 tablespoons) butter, at room temperature

2 tablespoons finely chopped cilantro leaves

1 shallot, finely chopped

1 teaspoon red chile powder

Cilantro Corn Bread

XXXXXX

Serves 4–6

3 strips bacon

1½ cups cornmeal

½ cup all-purpose flour

¾ teaspoon salt

2 teaspoons baking powder

1 cup shredded
pepper Jack cheese

⅓ cup thinly sliced
green onions

2 tablespoons finely
chopped cilantro

2 eggs

1¼ cups milk,
buttermilk, or yogurt

Feel free to add jalapeños or chopped roasted green chiles if you like.

Preheat the oven to 425 degrees F.

In a cast-iron skillet (or other heavy-bottomed, ovenproof skillet), cook bacon until crisp. Remove and drain on paper towels. Do not drain the bacon grease from the pan.

In a large bowl, combine the cornmeal, flour, salt, baking powder, cheese, green onions, and cilantro.

In another bowl, beat together the eggs and milk.

Add the liquid ingredients to the dry ones, until just incorporated.

Pour the batter into the cast-iron skillet (it should still be very warm), and bake 18–20 minutes, or until a toothpick inserted into the middle of the corn bread comes out clean. Serve hot.

Green Rice

xxxxxx

Serves 4

½ onion, diced

2 tablespoons olive oil

2 cloves garlic, finely chopped

1½ cups long-grain white rice

3 cups high-quality, low-sodium chicken or vegetable broth

½ cup finely chopped cilantro leaves

½ cup finely chopped parsley leaves

Salt

This brightly colored rice is very pretty. Use it for its flavor, but also to liven up a meal that would otherwise be visually unappealing.

In a saucepan over medium heat, sauté the onion in the olive oil until softened. Add the garlic and sauté 1 more minute. Add the rice and stir until the rice is coated with oil and heated through. Add the chicken stock and bring to a boil.

Cover the pan, reduce heat to low, and cook for 20 minutes, or until tender. Remove from heat, stir in the cilantro and parsley, and add salt to taste.

Sesame Noodles

xxxxxx

Serve these noodles with roast chicken or pork, and stir-fried baby bok choy. They are also very good served cold the next day.

Bring a large pot of salted water to a boil and cook the pasta according to the package instructions.

Meanwhile, in a large bowl, whisk together the peanut butter, tahini, soy sauce, peanut oil, and sesame oil.

Drain the pasta and add it to the peanut butter mixture. Toss to coat and season with salt, if necessary. Garnish with green onions, cilantro, sesame seeds, and red pepper flakes to taste.

Serves 6–8

1 pound spaghetti or Chinese egg noodles

$1/2$ cup creamy peanut butter

$1/2$ cup tahini (see Sources, page 77)

$1/3$ cup soy sauce

2 tablespoons peanut oil

1 tablespoon toasted sesame oil

Salt

$1/2$ cup sliced green onions, for garnish

$1/4$ cup finely chopped cilantro leaves, for garnish

1 tablespoon toasted white and/or black sesame seeds, for garnish

Red pepper flakes, for garnish

Spanish Black Beans

xxxxxx

Serves 4–6

¼ cup olive oil

½ cup chopped onion

½ cup chopped green bell pepper

½ cup chopped red bell pepper

3 garlic cloves, finely chopped

2 teaspoons ground cumin

2 tablespoons tomato paste

4 cups cooked black beans

1 cup high-quality, low-sodium chicken broth

¼ cup chopped green onions

¼ cup chopped cilantro leaves

The flavor of these black beans continues to improve after a day, so you may want to make them ahead and reheat just before serving.

In a heavy-bottomed saucepan, heat the olive oil and then sauté the onions and the green and red bell peppers until softened.

Add the garlic, cumin, and tomato paste, and stir to combine. Add the black beans and broth, bring to a boil, and then reduce the heat and simmer 20 minutes.

Stir in the green onions and cilantro. Serve with Migas (see page 64) or Roasted Chicken with Cilantro-Lime Rub (see page 57).

Cornmeal Crepes with Creamy Mushroom Filling

xxxxxx

For a very special presentation, make these into "beggars' purses." Put a few tablespoons of the filling in the center of the crepe, gather up the sides and tie into a purse-shape with a strip of green onion.

In a large bowl, combine the cornmeal, flour, and salt. Break the eggs and extra yolks into the cornmeal mixture and whisk to combine completely. Whisking constantly, add the milk a little at a time. Allow the batter to rest in the refrigerator while you make the mushroom filling.

Brush a cast-iron skillet or non-stick pan with a little melted butter. Add a few tablespoons of batter to the pan and tilt to spread the batter thin. When the surface of the crepe is pitted, flip it and cook until browned on the other side. Stack the cooked crepes on a plate kept warm in the oven.

Fill each crepe with some of the mushroom fillling and serve hot.

Serves 4

½ cup white cornmeal

¼ cup all-purpose flour

¼ teaspoon salt

2 eggs

2 additional egg yolks

1 cup milk

2 tablespoons butter, melted

1½ cups mushroom filling (recipe follows)

MUSHROOM FILLING

In a heavy skillet, melt the butter and sauté the onion until softened. Add the mushrooms and cook them until they turn from dry to wet.

Add the cream and simmer until the mushrooms are cooked through. Remove from heat and stir in the cilantro. Add salt to taste.

2 tablespoons butter

½ cup diced onion

1½ pounds mushrooms, cleaned and sliced

½ cup heavy or light cream

¼ cup finely chopped cilantro

Salt

Southwestern Mashed Potatoes

XXXXXX

Serves 12

3 pounds Yukon Gold potatoes, peeled and roughly chopped

1 cup shredded Cheddar cheese

¹/₂ cup sour cream

¹/₂ cup chopped cooked bacon

¹/₂ cup finely chopped green onion

¹/₃ cup finely chopped cilantro

Salt and freshly ground black pepper

Make these for a crowd. Even people who say they hate cilantro will love this dish. Try adding some chopped chipotles in adobo *sauce if you have them handy.*

Put the potatoes in a large stockpot and add enough water to cover. Cook about 15 minutes or until the potatoes are tender when pierced with a fork.

Drain the potatoes and return them to the hot pan, allowing any water left to evaporate.

Mash the potatoes by hand or with an electric mixer, adding the cheese, sour cream, bacon, green onion, and cilantro. Season to taste with salt and pepper and serve immediately.

In recent years, most decent-size grocery stores have responded remarkably well to our increased interest in ethnic foods. Look closely and you will probably find ingredients like hoisin sauce, canned chipotles, and tahini in the same store you shop at every week. Natural foods stores stock nearly all of these items, along with excellent selections of meat and seafood. Local ethnic markets will reward you with much more than you expected to find. If you have access to none of these stores, try these Internet sources:

SOURCES

Native American, Southwestern ingredients
(hominy, chiles, piñon nuts, etc.)
www.cookingpost.com, 888-867-5198

Middle Eastern ingredients
www.daynasmarket.com, 888-532-9627

Asian ingredients
www.asianfoodgrocer.com, 888-482-2742

INDEX